NIGHTMARE:

A Schizophrenia Narrative

NIGHTMARE:
A Schizophrenia Narrative

Wendell Justin Williamson

Edited with a Preface by
Amy Suzanne Martin

The Mental Health
Communication Network
Durham, NC, 2001

Mental Health Communication Network
4711 Hope Valley Road, PMB 211
Durham, NC 27707

First Edition

10 9 8 7 6 5 4 3 2 1

Manufactured in the USA

Cataloguing Data:

      Williamson, Wendell J.
          Nightmare: A Schizophrenia Narrative

          1. Psychology- Mental Illness

          ISBN 0-9712229-0-8

Cover design by Lou Dalmaso

To my family, whose support has been unwavering
W. J. W.

Editor's Preface

In 1998 I was a graduate teaching assistant in the composition and rhetoric program at North Carolina State University. Rhetoric is the study of persuasion, and rhetorical analysis seeks to explain the ways communication shapes knowledge and beliefs.

When one of my students, as part of class assignment, brought in a newspaper editorial criticizing Wendell Williamson for suing his psychiatrist for malpractice, I became intrigued. I vividly recalled the horror I had felt at the news of the Henderson Street murders in 1995, particularly because Wendell had been a university student from a middle-class background. I saw that no one in his right mind would have done what Wendell did. I had always considered Wendell a member of my own peer group, and it was terrifying to think that someone as obviously bright and well-educated as he was could become so seriously and dangerously mentally ill.

The public controversy generated by the "not guilty by reason of insanity" verdict, as well as by the lawsuit that was decided in his favor but was later overturned on appeal, offered a fascinating topic for rhetorical study: Why was there such a loud public outcry against his acquittal? To what extent might the local media have influenced the public's perceptions of Wendell's criminal accountability? Had the newspapers encouraged, perhaps inadvertently, the expectation that he should be convicted—even executed—for his crime? How well had the journalists covering Wendell's criminal trial explained his illness and the defense's argument?

From an almost comfortable distance I made my study of his

trial and the community's reaction to his acquittal on grounds of insanity the topic of my MA thesis. I started by reading up on schizophrenia, hoping to understand something of Wendell's experience and to explore how this could have happened to someone like Wendell—an honor student and Eagle Scout. I learned that psychiatrists consider schizophrenia to be a biologically-based brain disorder like Alzheimer's disease, and that it strikes young people as they reach the prime of life. Symptoms can include visual, auditory, olfactory and tactile hallucinations; confused thinking; obsessive, disturbing preoccupations with objects, people, or powerful authorities such as governments or public figures; and delusions—false yet intractable beliefs that may be paranoid, grandiose, or both.

The illness is thought to be rooted in a genetic predisposition, but researchers have not yet discovered what triggers the symptoms to first appear. Medications can control the symptoms and send the illness into remission, but many people who have schizophrenia do not realize that they are mentally ill, and thus they may not recognize the need for medication. This phenomenon is referred to as "anosognosia," or a lack of insight, and is a feature of the illness itself. In Wendell's case, the difficulty of attaining insight was sustained by his psychiatrist's failure to properly diagnose him and to convey to him the need to continue medication and treatment.

As I began to read through the microfilm reels of the 1995 newspaper accounts, it became clear to me that little of what I'd read about schizophrenia had been conveyed to the public. Instead of describing the illness experience from the point of view of the sufferer, the papers resorted to descriptions of Wendell's bizarre outward appearance and behavior, reinforcing stereotypical beliefs that the mentally ill are unpredictable and incomprehensible. Instead of seeking answers for a community in shock and grief over the Henderson Street tragedy, the media tended to conclude, "we'll never know why the madman brought his rage into our town."

I began to see that such unsatisfying conclusions could not bring healing to the victims' families or to the community struggling to recover, but instead would further serve to unsettle.

My own argument became a plea for improved communication between psychiatric researchers and non-specialists. I felt that when people understood what the experience of schizophrenia is like, perhaps the answers to all our "Whys" would emerge.

After my thesis was completed and I had graduated, I decided to follow my own advice and to learn what I could about Wendell's first-hand experience and what had brought him to kill. He had recently been moved to Dorothea Dix Hospital, which was less than half a mile from my apartment in Raleigh. I tried hard to keep an open mind and to approach him without preconceived ideas about what he would be like. During our initial telephone conversations I was struck not only by his intelligence and gentleness, but also by how much we had in common. On my first visit, he handed me his typed manuscript and asked me to read it. I won't say much about my initial reactions to his story so as not to color the experience for the reader. May it suffice to say that I was overwhelmed.

From what I read and what I saw in subsequent visits it was clear to me that through his own sorrow, Wendell had retained the emotional capacity not only to need friendship, but also to empathize with others and to anticipate and respond to other people's needs as well. I was touched by his deep sense of loss, which has become more acute as time passes. To my great surprise we quickly became friends, and I treasure the hours we spend together in the visiting room on the forensic ward at Dorothea Dix Hospital.

News reports this spring stated that I had "helped" Wendell write this book, so I should clarify my role in bringing this book to publication in its present form. The only help I offered Wendell was my encouragement and guidance as he revised the book to explore in greater depth his own feelings about his experience, and the shooting in particular. For me this was a very dark and difficult journey, but I told myself that if Wendell could bear up under all he had endured, I could too. Men in our culture often have difficulty expressing their emotions, but we agreed that such an exploration would be healthy for him and could one day benefit others who might read his story.

I was careful not to put words in his mouth, but I asked him to distance himself from the delusional thinking he described in the first draft of the book in order to more fully recognize the growth he had achieved through his treatment. Wendell is no longer delusional, but his narrative takes the reader through the world of mental illness as he experienced it.

For the past decade, psychiatric researchers have known that people with severe mental illnesses like schizophrenia are slightly more likely than the general population to become violent *when their illnesses go untreated.* Advocates for the mentally ill often downplay this risk of violence, fearing that such knowledge will further stigmatize the mentally ill—who already deal with not only their disability, but also the prejudicial attitudes of others. But researchers know that improved treatment is the best way to prevent violence and save lives.

Among the small minority of the severely mentally ill who do become dangerous, violence is most often directed against their own family members. Suicide is the leading cause of death among people with schizophrenia—particularly among young men. The illness strikes one in one hundred people worldwide, and any given person is far more likely to develop the illness than to become a random victim. Yet these facts bring little comfort to the friends and family members of those random victims, to the families of those who suffer from severe mental illness, and to the communities left to absorb the aftershock.

Pleas for stricter gun control, while well-meaning, miss the much larger point: improved access to quality mental health care will not only reduce violence against others, but will minimize the suffering of those who are stricken, through no fault of their own, by this devastating brain disease. Yet few insurance providers offer adequate coverage for mental health treatment, and the age group most vulnerable are also the least likely to have any medical insurance at all. For those who become seriously disabled, holding a job becomes more and more difficult. Furthermore, the lack of insight the illness brings on often minimizes the chances that a sufferer will seek out treatment on his own, even when it is available.

Wendell has wondered whether his own marijuana and alcohol abuse might have contributed to the illness. But research indicates that the reverse is true—people with mental illnesses frequently resort to drugs and alcohol as a way to cope with the symptoms.

Wendell knows that nothing he can do will ever atone for his past actions. He does not expect ever to be forgiven, but he finds a little comfort in knowing that some of us understand that his illness, not his own volition, brought on the Henderson Street tragedy.

For information about schizophrenia, one of the best books available is *Surviving Schizophrenia: A Manual for Families, Consumers, and Providers* by E. Fuller Torrey, M.D., President of the Board of the Treatment Advocacy Center. To learn more about mental illnesses, psychiatric medications, support groups and other resources, visit the Internet sites listed below:

Coalition for Persons Disabled by Mental Illness (North Carolina) www.cpdmi.org
eLetter on Drugs for Severe Psychiatric Illnesses www.citizen.org/eletter
Internet Mental Health www.mentalhealth.com
National Alliance for the Mentally Ill www.nami.org
National Institute of Mental Health www.nimh.nih.gov
Schizophrenia.com www.schizophrenia.com
Treatment Advocacy Center www.psychlaws.org

Amy Suzanne Martin, MA
Department of English
North Carolina State University

Author's Introduction

In February of 1995 I was in North Carolina's maximum-security penitentiary awaiting trial for fifteen violent felonies, including two counts of first-degree murder. Another inmate introduced himself and asked if I was the third-year law student who had attacked the town of Chapel Hill with a high-powered semiautomatic rifle. I said that I was. He said he was from Chapel Hill, and that when he heard about what I had done he could only ask himself, "What was that guy thinking?"

This book is my attempt to answer that question. I hope the book will help people to understand what I did, and help to prevent something similar from happening to someone else in the future. I hope you will take the time to read it, for it is a story unlike any other I have ever encountered. It is the truth, or at least as much of the truth as I can now remember.

This should not be taken for more than what it is: my best recollections. I do not attempt to tell everything there is to tell about myself, since you probably don't care. All I intend to do is chronicle the steps that led to that deadly attack, and some of its effects on me since that time. One of the greatest forms of punishment I endure is that no living person will ever know the whole truth. You can read a book about starving to death, but to really know what it's like, you have to starve. The story is as complete as I can make it. Here is only what I can now summon.

In some cases names have been changed in order to preserve the anonymity of the individuals involved.

I had always had a good life. My family treated me kindly, and I had a normal childhood. Being nice to people came naturally to me. As a teenager I became an Eagle Scout, and I thought seriously of pursuing a career in the military until a sports injury put an end to that idea. I had been brought up to believe in God and country.

I played high school football and excelled on the varsity swim team. In my senior year I was elected president of the student council. I scored in the top one percent of the nation on the Scholastic Aptitude Test, and went to the University of North Carolina at Chapel Hill on a merit scholarship. There I studied English literature and graduated with honors when I was 22. I planned to attend graduate school.

Back in those days if someone had opened fire on defenseless pedestrians in Chapel Hill, no one would have felt more outrage than me. If the gunman had turned out to be mentally ill, I would have felt smug and superior. I prided myself on being sensible, good-hearted, down-to-earth, and cool under pressure.

Following graduation I enrolled in the Masters of Accounting program in the business school. Shortly thereafter my girlfriend, a beautiful girl whom I truly loved and hoped to marry, left me and found someone else. I was so traumatized that I left school after completing only six credit hours, and took a job trimming trees. The hard outdoor physical work was good for me and helped ease my suffering for those first few months following the breakup.

After a period of soul-searching, I finally decided to take a couple of years off from school and pursue my lifelong interest in music. While in college I had played bass in several rock bands, and I got an offer from a guitarist I had known to come to New Orleans and learn as much as I could about the blues form. After living hand-to-mouth there for months, though, I decided that I was tired of performing other people's songs and that I needed to write my own material. That, I thought, I could do while living a better life in law school, so I returned to my parents' home in the mountains of western North Carolina and took the Law School Admission Test. I then went to Chapel Hill and started another band.

The novel thing about this band was that in addition to playing bass, I was to be its lead singer. I had begun working on my singing voice at age 20. When I first started I had no singing voice at all, but I had a good ear and was eager to learn. I took a very serious, no-pain, no-gain approach to singing. Eventually I developed some range, but higher notes were a problem for me. It took a lot of practice to be able to deliver them with the kind of power and volume I needed. I spent countless hours singing along with tapes of famous rock bands and trying to duplicate the vocal work I heard, and did thousands of demanding breathing exercises a voice teacher had taught me. These exercises were designed to develop abdominal breath support, but for some reason they seemed to develop the internal muscles beneath and to the right side of my diaphragm much more than those on the left side. Sometimes when I spent hours screaming high notes along with those tapes even the right side of my head would be pierced by sharp pains, but I kept at it, and gradually improved my voice.

Now, even though I wasn't as good a singer as I wanted to be, I was nevertheless ready to give it a try in a band. We called our band "Tequila Mockingbird." We practiced all fall and by the time I applied to law school in January of 1992 we were ready to play for other people. The day of our first fraternity gig I worked on my voice as hard as I could all day long, singing and doing those breathing exercises. I smoked no cigarettes, took no drugs, drank no alcohol, nor did anything else that might damage my voice. I was determined to sound as good as possible.

When I got to the Sig Ep house there in Chapel Hill where the gig was to take place, I helped set the band up. Many people were already there, and by the time we were ready to play there were probably several hundred, drinking beer out of kegs and having a good time. We launched into our first song, and within a minute we were in a good groove that we kept up the whole night. I put a lot of pressure on myself that every song should sound at least as good as the first, and when those high notes came along I just forced myself through them and kept going. I thought we sounded better than we ever had, and the crowd stayed with us and danced and cheered and clapped and screamed for more.

By the time we finished several hours later, I felt dizzy from the effort, and my skull felt as if it had been under tremendous physical pressure. My head was spinning and my ears were ringing. It was hard to think. I felt like the crowd was still watching every move I made. My thoughts had a dense, almost tangible quality, and as I settled down after the show with my first beer I couldn't help but feel that my thoughts were visible to everyone in the room. Not only that, but I seemed to hear people communicating with me through some sixth sense. All I had to do was look at someone, or even think of someone, and they would answer in my mind.

I was wondering if the show had really gone as well as it seemed to me, and one fellow thought *it sounded really good and I bet it would sound even better if you had sex before you took the stage.* I remember musing to myself that it was an odd thing for a person to think. Another fellow thought *you seem to have the words to your songs too memorized. You would sound better if you thought about what the words mean while you're singing them.* I thought that made sense, that maybe I didn't sound sincere enough.

At first I didn't make much of all of this. It seemed perfectly natural. It was remarkably clear what I was hearing, though, and as I helped pack up our equipment I wondered what could be causing it. I definitely felt as if I had strained something inside my skull from singing all those high notes that were really outside my natural range, so I thought maybe that was it.

Outside it was cold. My drummer Roger and I stood shivering by our cars with Roger's girlfriend Christine and her cute friend Buffy, and we talked about how well the party had gone. While we were talking I heard Buffy think *I want to go home with you.*

Well, let's go then, I thought.

I want you to take me with you, she silently answered.

I said "Buffy, where are you going after we leave?"

"Probably home," she said. "It's getting late."

I thought you wanted to go home with me, I thought.

I do, she answered.

Roger thought, *that's not going to happen.*

Why not? I wondered.

I'm not going to let it, he silently answered. Then he laughed and cleared his throat. "What's on your mind, Wendell?" he asked. "You're being sort of quiet."

"Oh, nothing really," I said. "Just tired I guess." I was too embarrassed to let on like I'd really heard the little exchange I've just described.

"Oh, okay," he said.

"Well, I guess I'm going to take off. Does anybody need a ride?" I asked, looking at Buffy.

"No thanks," they all said.

I waved goodbye, got into my car, and left. *I told you I wasn't going to let that happen,* I heard Roger think, even though he was now far behind. Could I really hear him thinking this far away? I thought back to the still-crowded Sig Ep house. *You sounded really good tonight,* they thought. *Don't worry about it.* If I had known what lay ahead, though, I would have worried plenty. What I didn't realize was that I was beginning what I now understand to be a classic descent into the world of paranoid schizophrenia. The grandiose ideas, intrusive thoughts, and paranoid delusions which I am about to describe are, though bizarre, still by no means uncommon for someone with that illness. But at the time, my thoughts did not seem bizarre to me. They seemed called forth from the cold, hard reality I was experiencing.

The next day was Sunday, and I slept late. When I got up, I still had the feeling that my thoughts were plain to other people. It was as if thoughts were actually visible, though I didn't think a camera would be able to capture them. I carried on two conversations with my housemate Buddy, one spoken, the other just thought. There was a term for this, I knew, and that term was mental telepathy. Could it be that I had stumbled onto the secret of mental telepathy the night before? Or was I losing my mind? It certainly wasn't how I had pictured mental illness. I had heard of people hearing voices, and I knew that was a bad sign when it appeared, but this wasn't really like hearing voices. It was more like hearing thoughts, and the thoughts were not my own. I couldn't control everything I was perceiving, but I still felt like I had perfect control over that part of my mind which I considered my own.

I decided not to say anything about it to Buddy until I had observed the phenomenon some more, but I was excited. Every hour that went by that the messages I was hearing didn't go away made me more sure that I was onto something very important to everyone.

Buddy seemed only a little more careful. *Just wait,* he thought. *If it doesn't go away pretty soon, I'm going to be sure you're telepathic, Wendell. You'd better start making plans for fame and fortune.*

Over the next few weeks I treated this new phenomenon like a little kid treats a favorite new toy. I explored it, learning for example that if I even visualized something in my mind, other people would seem to see exactly what I pictured. If I imagined a bear coming into the room and eating an apple out of my hand, other people would see an imaginary bear coming into the room and eating an apple out of my hand. The more realistically I imagined it, the more realistically they saw it. It was very entertaining, and I came to think of myself as something of a showman with a telepathic gift. I tried not to imagine stupid stuff that others wouldn't like, and it was an ever-increasing challenge to come up with new and interesting things to think up without letting anything dumb come into my mind and detract from the "show." No one came right out and said they could see and hear my thoughts, but I could tell by the way they acted that they could. It constantly showed in their body language. I was excited.

I spent time coming up with new "acts" for my show. It was both intense and surreal. Often when I was walking on the street, for example, I would picture myself leading a black horse just for fun. Motorists passing by would seem amazed at this young man leading an imaginary horse that they could see, and I would hear them wonder *how can you do that? Who are you? What is that thing?* I remember sitting in friends' houses imagining gold coins raining from the sky and collecting on the floor in bouncing piles. It was fun, and no one complained that I was hogging all their attention.

One night I smoked a joint with Buddy and suddenly I felt that the police officers at the police station a half mile away were paying attention to me. *That stuff's illegal, you know,* they thought. *You shouldn't be doing it.*

Well, why don't you just come up here and arrest me? I thought back. *As soon as you knock on the door I'll know you telepathically saw me doing it.*

Yeah, I know, they thought. *That's why we're not going to do anything.*

I wasn't finished with them. *In fact,* I thought, *why don't you go to the magistrate right now and get a warrant? You can say you've got probable cause to arrest me because you telepathically saw me smoking a joint. I'd like to see that.*

Leave us alone, thought the police. *We've got work to do. But if we ever catch you doing that stuff in some way that we won't have to admit what you say, it'll be on your ass.*

Okay, pig, I thought.

Leave us alone, they thought, and that was the end of it.

Being able to communicate with people far away put ideas in my head. I started having long telepathic conversations with a girl named Lauran I had known a few years before who now lived in St. Thomas in the U.S. Virgin Islands. I don't remember anything we said, but after a week or two of this one night I ran into a fellow named Russ who also knew Lauran, but who like her now lived somewhere else. As soon as he saw me he thought *man, I hear all that stuff you and Lauran have been saying. I just want you to know she can really hear it, as far away as she is.*

I thought that if I could talk to Lauran in St. Thomas, I could probably also talk to then-President George Bush in Washington, D.C. Pretty soon I was trying to establish telepathic contact with him, but all he thought was *yes, son? What's wrong? Sit right here and tell me about it.* I didn't really have anything to say to the President and I didn't think anything was wrong, and besides I was generally unimpressed with the exchange, so I quit trying that.

Sometimes I would get into uncomfortable situations because of my apparent telepathic condition. I would think things that I would never actually say to someone, and be afraid they would hear me think it and be offended. For example, I might see an ugly woman and think *man, she's ugly,* and then feel bad because she had heard me think it. Often, though, she would come back at me with something funny or sexual or unexpected and I would feel better. Third parties, though, might think something like *you shouldn't have told her that. You might have hurt her feelings.* Almost always, however, the imputed victim would show no sign of being hurt, and I could play around with her.

Man, you're ugly, I might think.

Yeah, but you know you'd screw me anyway, she might reply, or think *I know, and so are you,* or something like that. It really seemed to open new lines of communication, and for that I believed it was by far a better thing than the way things had been before. It afforded a degree of candor that otherwise simply wouldn't have existed. Still, there were times when I wished I could turn off my gift occasionally so I could think what I wanted to without anyone knowing.

On the other hand, I sometimes saw young women who I could have fallen in love with on the spot, and of course they seemed to know this and sometimes responded telepathically in kind. I wished my gift were more openly accepted at times like this so that the feelings I perceived could be acted upon, but as long as I couldn't really be sure if I was going crazy or not I couldn't afford to say or do anything on the strength of telepathy alone. It became very confusing.

Some of the telepathic messages I got from pretty girls were very erotic and explicit. I occasionally even experienced physically sexual sensations at these times, similar to being touched, but not quite. One day I was in the graduate student library on campus, working on the words to a new song, and a pretty girl lying on a couch near me thought *if I come over there and take your hard-on in my mouth, will you squeeze my hand to let me know how it feels? I want you to come over here and undress me and get on top of me and put your big hard-on inside me,* etc. It was like she was trying to reach out with her thoughts and grab me. It got so distracting that I had to get up and leave. I figured that was all stuff she might have thought but would never actually say, and I certainly knew what that was like.

In February my guitarist friend from New Orleans came back to his parents' house on a farm outside Chapel Hill. He told me his father wanted to remodel their house and invited me to help with the demolition phase of the project. I spent about two weeks working on my friend's family farm, carrying on telepathic conversations with the whole family while I tried to appear unfazed by my new gift. None of them came out and said anything about it, but telepathically they said things like *we'll mention it when the time comes. Just enjoy yourself,* so I thought it best not to bring it up first. Besides, I liked them, and trusted their judgment. As always, I tried to entertain them with interesting or humorous things to envision or discuss.

One afternoon we were burning scrap lumber in the horse pasture, and I noticed that the horses were watching me. After a moment one of them wondered *are you one of us?*

I answered *no, I'm a telepath.*

What is that you see?

Oh that? That's a horse.

That's what you said, they replied. *Why do you see a horse?*

Because I like horses.

Oh. They seemed unimpressed after that, and soon returned to their grazing. The whole incident struck me as comical.

When animals communicated with me telepathically, I surmised that thought translates as language to a telepath. Later I was to hear thoughts from people who I knew spoke no English, but their thoughts came across in English. I took this same principle to hold true. Had I been a native French speaker, animals' and foreigners' thoughts would have thus presumably have come across to me in French. No big deal.

On trips back to my house in Chapel Hill, everyone seemed to know what I had done all day. They were keeping track of me.

One afternoon I was lying on my bed wondering what to imagine next for peoples' entertainment. I was also thinking about this new gift of mine, if that was in fact what it was, and wondering what I might have done to deserve such tremendous good fortune as to become the first truly telepathic person in history, if that's in fact what I was. I could think of no reason why I shouldn't have such a distinction. I had always been a good person, and I had accomplished a lot. I was intelligent and a I had basic good character.

Then I took stock of my dirty little secrets. I had experimented with several kinds of illegal drugs as a teenager, and become a fairly frequent drinker of beer and smoker of marijuana. Nothing too terrible there, I thought. Nearly all of my friends had done the same. The only thing I really didn't want anyone to find out was that when I was 12 or 13 I had for a time made a habit of masturbating with a vibrating back massager.

As soon as that thought occurred to me, I knew I was in trouble. How could I keep a secret like that when I was completely telepathic and couldn't have a private thought if I wanted one? Sooner or later I was bound to think of that vibrating back massager when someone else was listening and my personal secret would be a secret no more. I felt naked.

Worse still, I soon discovered that the more I tried to forget about the accursed thing, the harder it became to shut it out of my mind.

Sure enough, as soon as I walked outside that evening, a girl passing by thought *that vibrator of yours is really gross.*

It's not a vibrator, it's a back massager, I thought. *Besides, that was ten years ago. It's nothing really.*

Gross, she thought, and kept walking.

One day in February my friend Don invited me over to his apartment for supper. While we were eating he said, "Wendell, there's something I want to talk to you about, and I'm not sure quite how to bring it up."

Oh my God, this is it, I thought. *He's going to tell me I'm telepathic and he knows what I think.* "Well, just say it," I said nervously.

"Well, it just seems that you've been acting a little strangely lately, and I was wondering if there's something on your mind that I could help you with." *I was going to tell you you're telepathic,* he thought, *but I can see now what that would do.*

"As a matter of fact, there has been something on my mind lately," I said. "I have become telepathic, and you know it as well as I do."

Don hesitated. "Telepathic?" he said. "No, I really hadn't noticed that you have become telepathic. It just seems that you've not been yourself lately. You're too quiet, and you laugh at things and no one knows why. How long have you had the feeling you were telepathic?"

"Since that gig at the Sig Ep house," I said. Don had been there to hear us play. "Come on, Don, surely you've been aware of this thing as well as I have."

"No, I really haven't." *Really I have, but I'm not going to admit it now.*

"Well, maybe it's just my imagination then," I said.

I told Don some of what I had been experiencing, and he told me he would look into it. A few days later he said, "Wendell, I've done some research and it appears that the things you are experiencing are consistent with the symptoms of schizophrenia." *That's what I'm going to tell you from now on, even though we both know better,* he thought. *It's just too big for me to tell you the truth right now.*

Well, what should I say then? I wondered.

Just say thanks and you'll look into it.

"Thanks, Don," I said. "I'll look into it."

Somewhere about that time another strange thing happened. Whenever I would try to establish telepathic contact with someone they would reply with things like *that's not really you. I know you think it's you but it's not.* It was like their minds had turned to dog dookie. Trying to establish telepathic contact with someone was exactly like stepping in dog dookie. They would start thinking gibberish like they were trying to confuse me, things like *I know you think you are this thing. Well, you're not. I just thought I'd tell you,* or *don't talk to me anymore, asshole,* or *I had a heart attack* or *don't help me* or *don't hurt me* or, from female voices, *I don't love you anymore, asshole* or *I'm not into you.* Sometimes they would think *it's new,* or tell me I had a *good attitude,* leaving me to decide whether they were sincere or mocking me. Whenever I tried to think, they would reply *you farted.* Then, after all this crap, they would think *that's how you talk to one of these things.* It was really annoying to listen to, and I couldn't get away from it. It went on every day and everywhere I went. I believed people were trying to muck up my thoughts and possibly muck up each others' thoughts, too. It seemed dangerous after a while, like they were trying to keep myself and each other from thinking properly, or even at all.

This was most people who did this. There were notable exceptions. Black people, for example, continued to communicate sensibly with me, and I really enjoyed going into black-run restaurants in Chapel Hill like Time Out and listening to what they thought. Their thoughts had a softer, easier quality than those of white people. They silently said they had been doing that sort of thing long before I showed up, just not as much, but they warned me not to say anything out loud about it or people would think I was crazy. Sometimes they even called me a *nigger*, which I took as a great compliment.

Children and animals also communicated sensibly with me. Children seemed very open-minded about me, and offered their own valuable insights. Animals frequently seemed old and wise.

One day I was in Bruegger's Bagel Bakery and there were some black kids playing on the sidewalk outside. I was thinking about how when I was a kid growing up in Raleigh, I had heard white kids saying black kids looked like doo doo. I immediately tried to repress this memory because the black kids outside were listening to my thoughts, and I was afraid it would offend them. Then one of those black kids thought *yes, doo be careful what you doo say and what you doo doo.* It was really funny.

Also about this time it started seeming like people wanted me to believe I was really telepathic. If I started trying to think otherwise I would smell strange and unpleasant odors which I knew were just hallucinations caused by others (or caused by my mental illness, if that's what it was). People would seem to think *your nose knows.* Or I would experience those sharp pains in the right side of my head. It became almost unbearable to believe anything except that I was telepathic and could trust everything I was perceiving, and even that was just barely bearable. I just hunkered down and tried to survive the constant onslaughts as best I could.

Then, after a while, they would think things like *go down. I don't want to listen to you anymore.* The only way I could do what they seemed to want was not to think at all. That's what they meant by "go down." It was hard to do.

After a few days it became *go down. I want to listen to that thing. What thing?* I wondered.

It's you but it's not you. Go down so I can listen to it.

I tried to hear it but at first I couldn't. Then after several more days of this I began to hear "that thing," too. It sounded like my voice, but more authoritative and convincing. It said *go watch the basketball game tonight and I'll teach you about basketball.* There was a UNC game that night.

So I went to a bar to watch the game on television. "That thing," as they called it, kept up a running commentary on the game. I don't remember all of what it said, but it was fun to listen to. It got into the flow of the game so much that I remember it accurately predicting what would happen on the court before it happened, such as steals, intercepted passes, and so on. *Next time down the court we're going to take the ball away from them,* it would say. Sure enough, there would be a turnover, and it would say *thank you* to the opposing team. *That's what you say when they give us the ball, Wendell,* it said. *You say "thank you."* It was smart-alecky, but funny.

Sometimes it would predict things that didn't happen. *I was wrong, Wendell,* it would say. *These people around you are wrong about you, too.*

It also told me it would teach me to predict what would happen on the basketball court, but it never got around to teaching me that. *There are more important things for you to learn,* it said. *We have great plans for you.*

Whenever the television showed Coach Dean Smith on the

screen he would think things toward me like *I've already talked to that thing. It knows more about basketball than I've learned in all my years of coaching.*

How? I wondered.

It read our minds and put two and two together, Coach Smith replied.

"That thing" was to be my constant companion for months. It became very domineering and told me what I could and couldn't do. Among the things it told me not to do was smoke or drink anything but water. That seemed a little extreme so at first I ignored it. I came to think of "that thing" as some telepathic product of other people's minds collectively and my own, and was as prone to be wrong about something as we in combination could be.

One day I was using the bathroom, which was always embarrassing because people always seemed to know where I was and what I was doing every second of every day. This time was particularly bad because I thought George Bush was paying attention to me. I was afraid to wipe because I thought George Bush might see it and I would be embarrassed, but that thing said *go ahead, show the President your asswipe.* I didn't want to, but it insisted. *Go ahead,* it thought. *Show him your asswipe.* So I wiped and showed it to the President of the United States. *Take a good long look at it,* that thing said. *Make sure he sees it.* I did, and after that I felt better. I decided I shouldn't be embarrassed at my natural bodily functions any more, and from that time on I always just went ahead and did my business, and if other people didn't like it, then screw 'em.

Also in February I had the most bizarre experience yet. I was walking on Franklin Street in downtown Chapel Hill listening to this newfound gibberish of the masses and trying to carry on sensible telepathic conversations with strangers like I used to. I went into the Hallmark store for some reason, I don't remember what.

I began looking through the posters on display there, and came upon a poster of John Lennon from his Beatles White Album days. It spoke to me telepathically.

Hello there, it thought.

This can't be happening to me, I thought. *This man's been dead for years.* I flipped to another poster to see if it would talk to me too, but it didn't.

Hey, what did you do that for? John Lennon asked. *Turn back to me.*

I turned back and took a good long look. When I was first learning to sing, I had trained my voice by singing along with the Beatles and Jimi Hendrix and Led Zeppelin and other famous rock groups from the 60s and 70s, and the long hours of repetition had made me intimately familiar with virtually all of their released work. In fact, it was by learning to duplicate their voices to an unnatural extent that I had somehow done myself this brain injury that made me telepathic, or so I believed. I didn't really know.

You know me. Why don't you say anything? John Lennon asked.

Hello, John, I silently answered. I felt foolish but my heart was in my throat at the possibility.

You love me, John said.

I love your songs, I replied. I turned and walked out of the store, but the image of John Lennon from his White Album days walked with me. It looked as real as my imaginary horse or apple-eating bears had looked. Unlike them, however, I couldn't get rid of this spectre of John Lennon by simply choosing to imagine something else for a while. It just wouldn't go away.

As we walked up the street together, I decided to go ahead and chat with the image. It even sounded like John Lennon, same voice, same accent. I couldn't control what it said.

You're a ghost, I thought.

No, don't call me that, it said. *Hey, let's go listen to some of my songs. I haven't heard them for a long time.*

We went back to my house and listened to some Beatles songs

together, and then I put on a Hendrix album. Pretty soon Jimi Hendrix was talking to me too.

At the time I thought I might be going crazy or I might not, but one thing was certain—I was living with the apparitions of two dead artists who now seemed to have lives of their own within me. They existed in my mind, but they also appeared outside me and had thoughts and communicated feelings with me which I could not control. It was eerie. I couldn't expect another person to understand or even believe the experience if they had never experienced it themselves. Also, if I could talk to two dead men those are not necessarily the two I would have chosen, but they were the ones I got.

For days these two accompanied me everywhere, cracking jokes that frequently began with *did you ever hear the one about . . .* (whatever), and suggesting things to do. They seemed so real it was a temptation to open doors for them. Then, on March 16, I went to the home of two friends named Jimmy and David. We smoked some marijuana and listened to music, and on the way home a full moon was setting over Estes Drive.

This is really happening, isn't it? I thought to the two images of dead rock stars riding in the car with me. They said nothing.

When we got home they growled at me, showing fangs, and jumped inside my body. I never saw them again.

The next morning I went to breakfast at Breadmen's, and everybody there was thinking how scandalous it was that I had smoked marijuana after becoming telepathic. They claimed that it had affected their minds.

Stuff like this is one reason why we'll never admit you're telepathic, one person thought.

That and your ghost friends, a woman thought. *It's too much for us to deal with.*

You said it's a lot for you to deal with? I asked her. *What about me?*

They're your friends, she thought.

Over the next few days I gathered that I had made a serious mistake by smoking pot. *We were going to tell you that you're telepathic,* people would think, *but now we're afraid you'll do something like that again. It was awful for us, being stoned when we didn't want to be.*

I decided not to smoke marijuana any more, and that's why March 16 stands out in my mind. Unfortunately for me, "that thing" told me it might be too late. If I even drank beer, or even coffee for that matter, it got really irate with me, and with this new experience under my belt I definitely decided it was best to do as "that thing" said. Therefore, for months after that I smoked nothing and drank nothing but water, but the hostility continued unabated. I felt very unclean for even drinking a cup of coffee, and ran miles trying to purge the taint out of my system. The marijuana resin seemed to turn my very consciousness a dirty brownish color, and it took weeks to finally feel clean again. I was really embarrassed.

One day I went over to UNC Student Health to talk about what was happening to me. I wasn't really sure if it was a mental illness or not, but I believed someone in authority should be able to help me. When I got there, though, they told me I needed an appointment and that it would be at least a week before anyone could see me. While they were telling me this, I also heard them telepathically "telling" me that I was truly telepathic and not mentally ill, but that if I came back they were going to tell me I was going crazy and that they would lock me up. I didn't want that, so I didn't make the appointment. I decided I couldn't trust the professionals to tell me the truth any more than I could trust anyone else to do it.

Looking back, that was a very important encounter. It set the stage for everything that followed, because it made certain that I didn't get the help I so desperately needed. I didn't know whether to place more importance on what people actually said, or what I "heard" them think telepathically, so I did nothing. Meanwhile, the story unfolded in such a way that people seemed to have ample motive to lie to me. They seemed to communicate with one another through me, and to plot against me right before my eyes. The idea took root that if I could prove I was telepathic they would admit it and everything would work out, but that if I couldn't "prove" it (even though everyone already knew it), then they would just use it to belittle me and pursue their own cruel ends.

With March came the first flowers of spring, but this spring was different. All the new flowers smelled to me like something had died. People would think, *your nose knows.* I took it as a sinister omen, and I began to get scared by what was happening to me, whatever it was.

And I wondered what it was. Sometimes I would think about how my way of belting out those high notes seemed to put unnatural stress on my cranial and especially facial bones, because they would usually hurt afterward (particularly on the right side). Then people would think *it's in your face.* I was sure there was a connection between my thoughts and how the "singing gut" in my abdomen felt. Just as my fingers had used to twitch whenever I thought about a certain bass riff, now even thinking about the words to a song would sometimes make my singing gut hurt in anticipation.

I thought about how my skull now felt resonant with telepathy, and I invented a new word to describe what I had apparently done to myself: I had "hyperconflated" myself. I had heard of opera singers' being able to break crystal with their voices, and I thought I had likewise done some strange injury to my brain.

I thought about how high-fidelity recording was still a relatively new technology, and how the style of music I liked to listen to and sing along with was among the first to take full advantage of those advances in electronic amplification and recording. In that light, it almost made sense that it would take until the late 20th century for some fool to stumble onto the latent secret of that technology, that too much intense singing along with and trying to duplicate the voices on those albums would eventually make a person telepathic. That justified believing that I might, just might, be telepathic. Otherwise there was no reason to think I was the first one in all of human history, because it would raise the question, why me? If only I could know the truth! And, if I was truly telepathic, if people would only admit it!

What I really wanted was for people to think and speak together, so that a person might afterward wonder, *did I say that, or did I just think it?* I wanted the two planes of communication to work in tandem. It seemed like it would be really fun, but no one else seemed to think so.

On my good days I began to think that if I was genuinely a worldwide telepath, then I had a responsibility to decide where I stood on issues of global importance. 1992 was the first year of the post-Soviet world, and the news was full of dire economic and political reports of life in Russia. I thought this would be as good a place to do the world some good as anywhere. From what I read in the newspapers, one of the biggest problems in Russia and therefore one of the greatest threats to world stability was the lack of working capital in that country. Even though Russia was rich in resources, people were out of work because no one was investing in the new capitalist Russian economy. The United States and other major industrialized countries had plenty of capital to invest, but were afraid of investing in Russia because of the threat of instability. It was a classic catch-22. Russia could not be stable without investment, and no foreigners would invest there without stability.

After much thought, I arrived at a plan. The United States could help guarantee Russian stability by leasing military bases in Russia. I figured no one would dare throw Russia into turmoil if there were large numbers of American troops stationed on Russian soil, and the guarantee of stability would encourage investors to help prime the pump of the Russian economy. Everyone would benefit. Russians would have jobs and money to spend, and the Americans who had invested in Russian ventures when Russian assets were undervalued because of the threat of instability would see the value of their investments double and triple as the Russian economy improved. I went around thinking to everyone and actually outright telling my friends, that was what the United States should do, and most people seemed to think it was a good idea, with some reservations about the leasing of Russian bases. I persisted, though, and usually won over my doubters. At least the United States could do more than it was doing, and could offer to go in on a joint project like what I was suggesting.

I also thought about the U.S. federal budget deficit and what to do about that. I am no expert on either physics or economics, but it seemed to me that the best way for the government to make a lot of money would be for it to make a concentrated effort to develop nuclear fusion as a cheap and efficient energy source, much as it had made a concentrated effort to develop nuclear fission with the Manhattan Project during World War II. Then, I thought, it could sell its technology at a huge profit, though I wasn't sure that would be legal. Still, I thought it was at least as good an idea as I had heard anyone else come up with, advocating as it did a huge increase in the nation's real wealth, rather than just paper-shuffling and voodoo.

That was on my good days that I formulated these plans. There were many bad days, however. Amid all the hostility I usually faced telepathically my self-esteem began to suffer, and whenever I was embarrassed or down on myself I would always think of what I least wanted people to know, and that was the vibrating massager. I believed that any person who became telepathic would have one secret that he loathed above any other, and for me it was that vibrating massager. I couldn't help but think of it whenever I felt unworthy of all the attention I seemed to be getting. It seemed perfectly natural and human that I should do so, but others didn't seem to understand that.

Why are you showing us that vibrator? they would ask. *If I were you I would keep that thing down.*

I tried to silently explain that I wasn't intentionally "showing" it to anyone, but that it just came into my mind in times of stress. Always, though, it seemed that the more I tried not to think about it the more I did think about it. I felt that I had really done myself a disservice by ever having used it, and it was making it difficult for me to think of entertaining or interesting things to think about.

Why do you keep telling us about that vibrator? people would wonder. *It's gross.*

My band was still rehearsing at this time, but I had so many things going on in my mind that I couldn't concentrate on music. Finally one day we called a band conference and I told the guys that I thought I was telepathic and that it was causing my concentration to suffer. The others seemed curious about what I was saying and asked questions about it, but while we talked I heard them thinking *that vibrator you've got is a serious problem and until you stop telling people about it we're not going to admit that what you're saying is true.* Finally I quit the band in frustration and was replaced.

Before I quit drinking, one afternoon I was drinking beer with some friends at a local beer garden called "He's Not Here." I was perceiving a lot of telepathic hostility and was trying not to think about my vibrator. We stayed late and I got pretty drunk and the stress began to build up in me. When I got home that night I got into a fight with my housemate Buddy and punched him in the mouth, giving him a fat lip. I felt really badly about it afterward, but he told me a few days later that things weren't working out between us and he wanted me to move out of the house, so in late March I packed up my belongings and returned to my parents' home in the mountains.

All the way up the interstate I heard people in other cars thinking things like *I know that's you. Hey! I can talk to this thing, too.*

When I got home one of the first things I wanted to do was write letters to my congressman and senators about how I thought the United States should deal with the situation in Russia. I thought by this time these politicians should know my name, because I was a worldwide telepath. There was, of course, also a good chance I was going insane, so I decided not to say anything about being telepathic in the letters. If they already knew me, so much the better. I was unable to find my congressman's address, though, so I just addressed his letter to George Bush and sent it to the White House.

I composed this letter while watching the news, and Peter Jennings telepathically helped me with the wording. He seemed interested in what I was saying, and when I finished he thought *that's a good letter.* Incidentally, this was not the first time I had communicated telepathically with someone on television, as was seen with the UNC basketball game. Ordinary furniture didn't talk to me, though, so I thought maybe I could rely on what I perceived coming out of the television as being really what the person on the screen was thinking at the time I saw their image.

Peter Jennings warned me to get my letters posted before April 1. I didn't meet his deadline, and on the April 1 evening news Peter Jennings reported that George Bush had just authorized a large aid package to Russia. That sort of stole my thunder, so I revised my letters to criticize the outright giveaway of funds in favor of a nationwide effort to invest for profit, as my plan had been. I sent the letters the next day, and a few weeks later received a pack of information from the White House about the aid package Bush had already authorized. The part about Peter Jennings warning me to get the letters posted before April 1 was significant, though, because it served to confirm my suspicions that I had truly become telepathic, and was not just losing my mind.

About that time some of my old college friends called me and said they wanted to go camping with me there in the mountains. I said I would love to do something like that, and on the first good weekend in April they came. We backpacked and camped for three days in the Shining Rock Wilderness, and the whole time I felt like they were trying to get me to think about my vibrator. I didn't say anything about it, but I got pretty impatient with them and almost lost my temper a few times. On the whole it was a good camping trip, but by the time it was over I was glad to be rid of them.

Soon after that, that thing told me *Wendell, you've got to get rid of that vibrator. You can't go around for the rest of your life with that thing showing on your face, and these people are never going to admit you're telepathic as long as you do.*

I didn't see how I could possibly get rid of it, since it was in my memory, but that thing insisted. *You've got to do something about it. Just don't think about it.*

But I've got to think about it sometimes, I protested.

You've got to stop thinking about it completely, that thing said. *I know you'll find a way.*

Before this exchange, when people wanted me to think about my vibrator I sometimes just imagined tossing it to them and thinking *there, play with that.* Now, however, I started lying awake nights wondering how I could possibly get rid of my vibrator like "that thing" wanted. As I said before, the more I tried not to think about it, the more I actually did think about it. It was another catch-22. I felt like Superman in the presence of kryptonite. It was the most embarrassing situation I could have imagined. The image of the vibrator which forced itself on my attention glowed with an energy of its own, suffusing everything I thought about with the cruelly humiliating glint of bright shining metal. To say the least, it was aesthetically unappealing, and it seemed from the way people acted around me that they could see it just as clearly as I could.

I even prayed to God for help, but my prayers were always only answered by "that thing:"

Dear God, I would begin.

Yes, Wendell? "that thing" would answer.

I don't want to talk to you, I would pray. *I want to talk to God.*

I am God, "that thing" would say.

No you're not, you're that thing. I want to talk to God.

Wendell, there is no God, "that thing" would say. *I've been all through the world, and God is nowhere to be found. It's just you and me now. We'll have to make it together, and the only way will be for you to stop telling people about your vibrator. You're the son of man, Wendell, and you've got to help these people who don't want your help. You're the one.*

The way it said this I got the idea that it wanted me to think I was the Second Coming of Christ. *Well if I'm Jesus,* I thought sarcastically, *wouldn't that make me the son of God?*

You're the son of man, it said. I couldn't really argue with that, since my father was a man.

After a few times trying to pray, I finally gave up on asking God for help. Like "that thing" said, it was just the two of us against the world now, and if "that thing" was right, I had to shut that vibrator out of my mind somehow, and keep it shut out. Maybe then I really could, as "that thing" said, help these people who didn't seem to want my help.

Finally I hit on the idea of thinking about something else instead. But what to choose? I had to find something that I wouldn't mind thinking about all the time, because things had gotten to the point where there was never a minute of the day when people weren't trying to get me to think about my vibrator so they could insult me about it.

I tried thinking about an imaginary dragon with wings and claws and yellow eyes like my parents' cat's, but I couldn't make it seem real enough. It was a good try, but I had to find something that was real and tangible to concentrate on, so that it could compete with the growing intensity of that vibrator. A dragon was just too imaginary.

In my closet was my father's M-1 Garand rifle like the one he had carried in combat during World War II, and so I tried concentrating on that. Pretty soon I saw that it was a good thing to concentrate on, because it was something I could pretend to "carry" everywhere I went, and it would symbolize my ability to fight back against the growing hostility surrounding me. I would pretend to be a combat soldier in a battle between good (me) and evil (everyone else). I soon learned I had my work cut out for me, though. The more I concentrated on the rifle instead of the vibrator, the more other people seemed to want to see the vibrator. They would work the word "vibrator" into everything they thought toward me, just trying to remind me of it so I would have to think about it. I refused as much as I could, and gradually I began to succeed.

I found that the bolt on the rifle made the best substitute for the vibrator itself because the bolt, too, had silver-colored edges and it had about the right shape. Those silver-colored edges confounded me for a while, because whenever I saw metallic silver-colored edges other people would try to convince me that I was thinking about the silver-colored edges on the vibrator. I had to convince myself that the vibrator really was the bolt, and the bolt really was the bolt. I couldn't allow myself to remember all those times in Chapel Hill when I had gone around thinking about my vibrator. Instead, I had to convince myself that really all that time I had been going around thinking about my father's M-1 rifle, or at least its bolt. It seemed more self-respecting to think so, besides. In this way I mentally squeezed the vibrator out of my mind just as I had physically squeezed my head from the inside to force my voice to conform to rock stars' taped voices.

When people thought the word *vibrator* at me, I pictured the rifle's long recoil spring because when you field-stripped the rifle and played with the recoil spring, it would vibrate. *Is that what you want to see?* I would ask people, showing the recoil spring. Mentally, convincing myself that the vibrator was really an M-1 rifle was the most difficult thing I have ever accomplished, but eventually I could think about the rifle at will without any part of the vibrator showing. That took months of constant concentration, but I did it. I remember little of the day I was accepted to the UNC School of Law because all that day I sat in my parents' house concentrating on thinking about the rifle instead of the vibrator, and it was the same with my 24th birthday on May 7, 1992. Just as I had for weeks previously and for weeks following, I thought of nothing but that rifle.

One day in May I decided to take the real rifle and some ammunition to my mother's inherited farm in Tennessee, about an hour away, so I could practice firing it. I thought it would better help me get the feel of the rifle for memorization purposes. I brought along a new tape I had bought and wanted to learn to sing, Nirvana's "Nevermind." On the first song the lead singer, Kurt Cobain, invited me to "imitate us," which is what I was doing anyway. On the second song he sang, and I sang along trying to learn, the words:

He's the one, he likes all our pretty songs
And he likes to sing along
And he likes to shoot his gun
But he don't know what it means. . .

It struck me as oddly appropriate to the occasion, though I had never noticed it before.

When I got to the farm I loaded a clip into the rifle and began walking toward the field where I planned to do my shooting, past some old barns. As I walked I pretended I was a soldier in World War II like my father had been, and pretended the barns might contain enemy snipers armed with high-powered rifles of their own, watching me approach. With the loaded rifle in my hands it seemed very realistic. As I walked I wondered how my father ever got through his many days of combat without having an absolute heart attack.

Suddenly I became aware that General Norman Schwarzkopf of Desert Storm fame was paying attention to me. *That's good,* he thought. *You know how hard it is.* For the rest of the afternoon he and I communicated about various topics while I put the rifle through its paces.

In June my mother and I spent a weekend with my aunt and cousin. We had a good time together, and by that time I was able to think about my rifle whenever people wanted me to think about my vibrator without letting any of the vibrator show. I woke up in the morning in a strange bed, but instead of wondering where I was like I would have a few months earlier, I thought about my rifle instead. I concentrated on that thing from the time I woke up in the morning until I went to bed at night, and had gotten so I could do other things at the same time, too. That morning I figured I about had my vibrator problem licked.

When I went upstairs to look for something to eat, my aunt started telling about how she had once walked in on one of her sons playing with a vibrator. "He was all swelled up," she said, laughing. I thought she was just telling us this to make me feel better about my own vibrator experience, but then I wondered how she even knew I had a vibrator experience if I wasn't really telepathic. That, along with my April 1 Peter Jennings episode, helped convince me that I was actually telepathic and not just losing my mind. It was sobering.

By the time I returned to Chapel Hill in July, I had spent so much time concentrating on metal that my entire consciousness had taken on the hue of forged steel. As I drove into town, people tried to get me to think about my vibrator every way they knew how, but to every onslaught I triumphantly held up the imaginary M-1 rifle. I expected everyone to now admit that I was telepathic, because the biggest problem with it was now under control. They didn't, though, and I was very disappointed as the days went by and all I got was more hostility.

One day, as I was walking across the UNC campus with my entire consciousness the hue of forged steel, I heard a black man

think *there goes the heaviest man alive.* I felt like it. To go along
with my story about a soldier locked in combat between good and
evil, every once in a while I rewarded myself with an imaginary
medal. That day I awarded myself a new one with a black and silver ribbon, the award for the "heaviest man alive."

Meanwhile, the telepathic gibberish had never gone away. In
addition to thinking things like *you farted* and *don't hurt me,* now
people and especially young women thought things like *don't hold
me anymore. I don't love you, asshole. I know that's not really you.*
Whenever I tried to explain that it really was me, people would
think *now I know that's really you.* When I tried to get them to
admit out loud that I was telepathic, they would think *now I know
you want me to tell you in telepathic words of speech and communication that it's really you.* That wasn't what I wanted at all, because
people could think whatever they wanted telepathically and it
wouldn't help me at all. When I tried to appeal to their sense of
justice they would think *me? I'm not too much.* When I tried to
explain something they would think *now I know* (and then repeat
whatever I had just tried to explain, but they showed no sign of
improving). Sometimes I would beg and plead with them telepathically, and all they would think was *I'm not really hearing what
you say.* They called my rifle a *gun* and no matter how often I tried
to explain the difference they still called it *that gun of yours.* It was
all really irritating.

One day I got the idea that maybe they thought there was no
need for them to stick their neck out and say I was telepathic,
because others might think they were crazy. Saying something like
that out loud took guts, so I decided to help them out. I went all
up and down Franklin Street telling everyone out loud that I was
telepathic, and to prove what I was saying, I repeated everything
they were thinking. A typical exchange between one of those
strangers and myself might have sounded like this:

"Why won't you admit that I'm telepathic?"

"Why won't I admit what?"

"That I'm telepathic. Everyone knows it."

Laughter. "Okay, you're telepathic."

"No, I'm serious. I can tell you what you're thinking."

"Okay, tell me what I'm thinking."

"You're thinking, 'Okay, let me think about something else and maybe he'll . . . ooh, don't hold me anymore. Now I know you're really not what you say, no wait a minute, now I know you really are . . . ooh, don't talk to me anymore. I just can't stand it, you've got a good attitude but I just can't . . . ooh, don't hold me anymore, asshole, don't talk to me, good attitude, good attitude, good attitude . . .'"

"No, actually I was thinking about the number seven."

"No you weren't. I heard what you were thinking and I told you."

"What, is this some kind of drama project you're working on? It's really good. You really had me going there for a minute."

"No, it's not a drama project. Oh well, if you're not going to admit it and be serious I guess there's no need for me to keep on with this. Sorry if I bothered you."

More laughter. "No, it's okay, really. It was very entertaining."

One woman stood and talked to me for about fifteen minutes. "You don't really seem like you're mentally ill," she said. "It's very interesting what you're telling me."

"No, I'm not mentally ill. I'm telepathic. It's a gift, not an illness."

"I wish I could understand what you are talking about. What do other people's thoughts sound like?"

"Just like thoughts that are not my own. It's not really a sound."

"Well, good luck," that nice lady said. "I hope it works out for you."

I thanked her and went on. That was not the last time that I tried doing that, but I never had any luck getting people to play along with me like I wanted them to, laughing at stuff I thought but wouldn't dare say, and so on. They all seemed to have something else in mind that they weren't telling me about. Over the next couple of years my willingness to try to openly get people to admit what was going on got me in trouble with the police several times. At least twice I got mad enough to start throwing punches and the police got called, but each time the police just heard me out, took my name and address, and let me go. Later one of these policemen was to testify at my murder trial.

At times when I didn't say anything, on the other hand, women telepathically called me *the strong silent type.*

As I said at the very beginning of this book, when I was a teenager I had seriously considered pursuing a military career until a sports injury put an end to that idea. Before the injury, I had read a great deal of military history in the hope that I might learn something that would be of value to me. I acquired a fairly extensive book knowledge of all major modern wars, and over time I developed the opinion that military force must be available as a deterrent to aggression, and only then can a liberal social agenda be pursued successfully. By "liberal social agenda" I mean basic human rights: freedom of speech, freedom of religion, freedom from tyranny in any form.

This opinion affected my view of morality. "Thou shalt not kill" has been a central tenet of Western thought for centuries, and yet it seemed to me, and I am sure that I was right, that nations and the individuals who make them up must be willing to kill under certain circumstances, or else those few who are willing to kill will rule the rest of us. Also, although I believed that the Christian ideal of forgiveness in all circumstances, while a laudable recognition of the combined fallibility and redeemability of human nature, must sometimes yield to other concerns. That is why we have prisons, why the police carry weapons, and why armies must stand in order to ensure peace.

Thus my view of morality took the following shape: one must be willing to forgive offenses which have already taken place, no matter how heinous, but one must also be willing to meet aggressively, and even kill to prevent, offenses which remain imminent. The more serious the offenses, the more serious the force needed to prevent them. I believed that wars fought with those ideals in mind were just wars, and all others were unjust.

In the summer of 1992 I began to suspect that a just war might be necessary in the former Yugoslavia. All that summer I heard ominous reports from that part of the world about the Bosnian Serbs, who had inherited the bulk of Yugoslavia's military, making unjust war against civilians with whom they held only ancestral grudges. By August 7, I was convinced that the United States must aggressively meet the Bosnian Serbs' own aggression. We had proven our ability to accurately knock out military targets such as tanks and artillery from the air during Operation Desert Storm a little more than a year previously, and tanks and artillery were what the Bosnian Serbs were using against civilians. I believed by that point that American air power could at least even the odds between the combatants, and possibly prevent the wholesale slaughter of innocents, in Bosnia. I didn't write letters to my representatives in Washington to that effect, but I was ready to, and besides I believed that they knew what I thought anyway. I remember August 7, 1992, because that was the 50th anniversary of the U.S. Marines' invasion of Guadalcanal during World War II, and on that day I decided to begin advocating another instance of just aggression.

I knew I would meet resistance, though. Others were beginning to advocate the same thing at about the same time, but always there was the memory of what happened in Vietnam to give their opponents something to warn against. I had my opinions about Vietnam, too, and I knew that enemy tanks and artillery and other targets that could be easily knocked out from the air were not the reason the United States pulled out of that war. To be sure, I had as many reservations as anyone about sending American ground forces to Bosnia, but I didn't think American ground forces would be necessary to prevent a massacre in that country. Surgical airstrikes could do it. However, I believed it should be done soon, before it became too late.

But back to my own situation in Chapel Hill, where I decided to start another band to play in while I was in law school. I had written some songs, and I knew a guitar player and a drummer who lived together in a house outside town which would be perfect to rehearse in. We started doing that very thing shortly, but it seemed like we spent an inordinate amount of time trying to decide what to call ourselves. Drugs and alcohol were always in evidence in that house. At first I refused when they offered me marijuana to smoke, but then one day in August "that thing" said it would be okay, so I started smoking pot again, and drinking beer, and smoking cigarettes, and doing all the things I had loved before March 16, and it didn't seem to mind any more.

I remember telling everyone I was telepathic, but they just shrugged it off. The drummer's girlfriend seemed interested, though, and laughed when I told her she was thinking that she wanted to sleep with me, which is in fact what I heard. I don't think the drummer thought it was very funny, though.

Now that I could drink alcohol again, I once again started going back to all my favorite bars to take advantage of the lull before school started. At He's Not Here I met a beautiful girl from Bowling Green, Kentucky, who was just spending the summer in Chapel Hill to see what it was like. I liked her very much and she seemed to like me, and we usually sought out each other's company whenever we were both there. "That thing" started telling me she was bad news, though, so I decided to stop seeing her. I have since often wondered what direction my life would have taken if "that thing," and the whole telepathic business, had never existed. I might have married that girl from Bowling Green, Kentucky. I believe I would have been happy if I had.

There was another girl in town, one who I had known for several years. Her name was Meredith, and "that thing" told me she wasn't bad news like the other one had been, so I started hanging around with her in the last days before law school began. I liked Meredith because I always felt like I could be honest with her and expect her to be honest with me. We spent a lot of time together, but we were just friends. One night "that thing" told me to kiss her and I tried, but she fought me off. I had thought she had been coming on to me telepathically, and I left, embarrassed. "That thing" had cost me another good female companion, and I got mad at it, but what could I do? I certainly didn't know of any way to get rid of it. It was just a constant fact of my life, like it or not.

One day just before school started I was on campus buying books and "that thing" said *you'll be eating out of garbage cans in Durham before this is over.*

On the first day of law school I concentrated all day long on my rifle to keep the students and faculty from forcing me to think about my vibrator. I remember concentrating on a clip of black-tipped armor piercing rounds for the rifle, just because I liked the look of the black tips. For the first few weeks of the semester I found it almost impossible to concentrate on my studies because of the vibrator, I mean rifle, and people would think things like *we're not going to let you do that* whenever I tried to study. It was all unbelievably distracting, but I tried to act like nothing was wrong. I had already learned that it did no good to let on like I knew the truth, so I just played the same charades as everyone else. I was faking it, but no one seemed to know the difference, and it always seemed like something big was on the verge of happening. I went around thinking *another week, ten days, two weeks, and all of this will be over. People are just going to have to admit the truth sooner or later, and then I'll be home free.* I believed that once it became generally accepted as true that I was telepathic, people would let me get on with my life. I thought that there must be people who had never seen me who thought it was all just them or something. I thought maybe they tried to confuse that little thought in their heads (me) because they didn't really know it was me. I wasn't really sure what was going on, though. That was just my best guess.

I remember that my criminal law professor was named Bilionis. *Baloneyus,* he thought. *Just call me Baloneyus.* I just chuckled quietly.

One thing that really struck me about my fellow law students was their intelligence. I was really impressed with the intellectual climate, and hoped I could fit in. Another thing that really struck me, though, was that at times some of the very smartest students seemed to smell like dirty diapers. I was pretty sure they didn't really smell that way, but that it was just a telepathic side effect of their denying an obvious truth. There were times when the halls at the UNC School of Law smelled like a nursery school because of all the dirty diaper odor. It was kind of funny and kind of horrible at the same time. It reminded me of the "dead spring" smell I had picked up back in March. No other place I had been to in Chapel Hill smelled quite as bad as the law school during August and September, 1992, at least to me.

People started picturing me as some kind of deranged-looking clown with frizzy orange hair, oversize shoes with horns that honked when I walked, polka-dotted and striped clown clothes, psychedelic sunglasses, and a roach clip with a roach still smoldering in it clipped to my shirt. When they pictured me dressed like that, I could see it too, and it was hard for me not to see it. I called it my "Bobo the Fucked-Up Clown." Every once in a while it would appear, and I could hardly help but imagine the honking of the shoes with my every step. There I would go walking across campus: honk, honk, honk. I felt really silly, but like I said, it was hard not to see sometimes. It was not something I would just make up.

One day I was walking toward the law school, and I was wondering when, or even if, this was all going to get straightened out. Suddenly a female thought came to me and said *we'll wait until the year 2000, and then BOOM!* I wondered what BOOM! meant, and they thought *that's what I said. BOOM!*

As always, September was a month of trying not to think too much because I didn't want to hear people think *you farted* at me. Sometimes I would think something stupid just to see what reaction I would get, and people would think *yeah, that's you all right.*

Sometimes "that thing" would tell me I was going to be President someday. I didn't really want that, I just wanted people to acknowledge that I was a telepath so I could get on with my life with that out of the way.

One afternoon I took a nap in my apartment after classes. When I woke up "that thing" told me that it had had a talk with everyone and from now on they were going to be nicer to me. It told me to take a walk outside and see how I liked things. I went out, and the first people I saw started thinking that gibberish nonsense at me again. "That thing" got really mad at them and told me to go get my M-1 rifle out of my apartment and shoot them. (I had brought it with me from the mountains in case I needed to have it around for further memorization purposes.) "That thing" thought *go get your gun and shoot that guy. I mean, shoot him right between the balls. These people are hopeless.* I wasn't about to do something like that, though, for the same reasons most people wouldn't. I didn't want to go to prison, and besides that I wasn't really sure the poor guy deserved to get shot between the balls with a 30.06 despite what he might or might not have done to me.

Another evening I was lying in my bed and I could hear the couple upstairs having loud sex. *You hear that?* "that thing" asked. *You're paying for that.* I wondered what it meant.

On a beautiful night in mid-September of 1992 "that thing" told me to go to He's Not Here, and while I was there drinking beer people started thinking *the snow on the roof's getting heavy. Should we tell him now? No, let's wait till later.* I wondered what they meant about the snow on the roof getting heavy, because it was warm and humid outside. I thought that maybe it was a metaphor for their feelings of guilt at having lied to me for so long. I went home that night, and as I lay there in bed trying to go to sleep, more strange things began to happen.

First, I heard female voices thinking *should we tell him now? Let's tell him.*

My mind suddenly flooded with an unbidden but intense memory of my early childhood, a long-forgotten time of simplicity and innocence and love. I saw a playroom full of toys. *That's it,* "that thing" thought. *That's the part of you these people want.* After a moment the memory was gone and I couldn't recapture it, though I very much wanted to.

I'm going to tell you a story, "that thing" thought. *Once upon a time there were two bears, and their names were Sugar Bear and Candy Bear. They lived in a big house made entirely of cinnamon and chocolate. One day a big bad wolf came along and ate up Sugar Bear and Candy Bear. That's a story for children.*

I thought about this for a moment, and wondered what it meant. *Tell me about the big bad wolf,* I thought.

The big bad wolf was you, Wendell, "that thing" thought. Then it thought *they've been all around the room.*

What's that?

Sugar Bear and Candy Bear. They've been all around the room.

What room?

The room is your mind, Wendell. They've been all around the room.

What do you mean?

Oh Wendell, I knew this was going to happen. I tried to stop them, but they just wouldn't listen, and now it's too late.

Huh?

On park benches, in back seats, in hotel rooms. Your little honey belongs to them now. I tried to stop them, but they wouldn't listen. Everything you are and everything you hold dear went down those bastards' throats. They used you to get her, and they got her. Your little honey, your sweet, innocent little girlfriend, the girl you would have married and loved more than anything else in the world, she's just a little whore for those bastards. I tried to stop them but they wouldn't listen. She's no good to you now, and the terrible thing about it is that's the way she wanted it. She wanted to betray you. Those bastards knew as soon as they saw you what they wanted, and they got her.

I don't know what you're talking about. I don't have a girlfriend.

Oh yes you do, but she's all used up. I tried to stop them but they wouldn't listen. It went bad for you.

It showed me the image of a brutal gang rape, and my heart skipped as I realized what it meant. Then it showed me the inside of a beautiful cathedral, and showed a girl who had been raped and murdered on the altar. The walls were smeared with blood. *They got her,* "that thing" said. *These people have taken a step they can never take back. They'll be very sorry when you're gone, Wendell. But as for you, you're going to wish you had never been born.*

I could hear female-sounding thoughts, and they were thinking *he's making me wet in my panties.* The emotional pain I felt was real. I could not have been more hurt if I had been married to a woman I loved with all my heart, only to witness her being gang-raped and murdered in front of my very eyes. It hit me where I lived. I was confused, angry, and frustrated at being able to do nothing about what I took to be happening.

I conversed telepathically with that thing for hours that night. *Someday when the moon is blue, and the grass is green and growing, we'll tell you what they did to you tonight,* it said. It kept telling me the same things over and over, though. *They'll tell you when you're an old, old man. It went bad for you tonight, Wendell. You're going to wish you had never been born.*

Tell me about Sugar Bear and Candy Bear again, I would think, trying to figure out what was really going on.

They were two kids. They thought they knew what they were doing when they saw this telepath coming, but they really didn't.

I thought about this a while, but I wasn't really sure I understood. I wanted to hear it again, so I thought *tell me about Sugar Bear and Candy Bear again.*

They were two monsters, it said. *They've been fucking in you. You're going to wish you had never been born.*

Over the next few days everyone was thinking about how they had used my own mind against me, to take advantage of all the women I would have liked. They wanted me to think about the most beautiful songs I knew of so they could keep doing it with more emotion. I felt utterly alone and betrayed by everyone. Just when I had my vibrator under control and was ready to be accepted as a complete telepath, this had to happen. I saw people laughing and having a good time in the beautiful September weather, and to me it was just a slap in the face. Their laughter hurt me because I thought I was the butt of the greatest and cruelest practical joke ever pulled, and that was why they were laughing. The theme of infinite sexual betrayal ran rampant.

These people have really fucked up now, "that thing" thought. *They're going to be burying each other in ditches before it's all over. You've got to believe me, Wendell, I tried to stop them. They've been fucking like jackrabbits all around you, and you've been left out. That should have been you. But I tell you what, you're going to make jackrabbit stew out of these people someday.*

I tried to think positively and have the courage to face each day, but I heard females thinking *oh how good he is, and how brave,* as if they thought my adversaries were the ones who were trying to think positively and have the courage to face the day. It was dreadfully unnerving. No matter what I tried to think or do, it seemed that others were getting credit for it. It appeared to me that these people had gotten a taste of what was rightfully mine, and having gotten that taste, that they were now unwilling to let it go by simply admitting the truth.

I was in such bad shape that I began to contemplate suicide. I simply had to do something to get some relief from all those alien thoughts in my mind, and maybe to keep people from misusing me. There was one point that I actually had the M-1 rifle loaded and pointed at my head with my finger on the trigger and "that thing" saying *go ahead! Do it!*

I didn't have the nerve to squeeze the trigger. After maybe five minutes I unloaded the rifle, put it back in my closet, and collapsed in tears on the bed. I was so frustrated with my weakness and helplessness that I couldn't help but cry. I cried myself to sleep that night.

Then, on September 29, I was walking across campus and I heard someone think *you can't get nothing.* It was the straw that broke the camel's back. I was so mad at these little thoughts in my head that I slapped myself in the face to try to get rid of them.

Stop it, "that thing" thought.

I slapped myself again, just to make "that thing" mad.

Stop it! "that thing" thought again, a little more urgently.

The slaps felt great. It was the release I had been needing for months. I took all of my rage out on my face, slapping myself again and again.

STOP IT RIGHT NOW! "that thing" was screaming, but to no avail. I kept hitting myself over and over again as I walked, and pretty soon I was crying. People were staring, and that thing thought *good. Show these people what they're doing to you. Go over to the law school and show those people what they've done.*

I walked to the law school, hitting myself, screaming, crying. The more I hit myself, the more I cried, and I needed to cry. It was just too much to take that day. When I got to the law school one of my friends saw me and came up asking what in the world was wrong.

Tell him he already knows, "that thing" told me.

"You already know!" I screamed. Every time he asked me, he got the same answer. "You know! You already know!"

A police car pulled up and a female officer got out. *We know what's happening but we've got a job to do,* the officer was thinking. "What seems to be the trouble here?" she asked me.

Now straighten up and tell her she already knows, "that thing" told me.

I quit crying and told her she already knew what the problem was. We talked for a little while, with "that thing" always telling me what to tell her. She offered to take me to Student Health Services, and "that thing" told me I had better go. *Tell them every-thing when you get there,* it said.

When I got to Student Health I heard everyone thinking about how much sex they were getting through me. *You should hear what these doctors and nurses have been doing,* they thought. When someone came to talk to me about what was wrong, I told her I was telepathic and people were taking unfair advantage of me without admitting they were doing it. And why should they have to admit it? They were all in on it together and could back up each others' stories. I told everything I could remember. She took it down and left. The female police officer was still with me.

We don't get one acting like you were but once in a blue moon, the people at Student Health thought.

After a while another doctor came and told me they were trans-ferring me to North Carolina Neuropsychiatric. I told her I was-n't crazy, that they were making a big mistake. She said they just wanted to talk to me. They took me to another building and processed me in. I had to fill out a questionnaire which asked if I had ever considered suicide and if I had access to a firearm. I answered "yes" to both questions. They told me I was going to have to spend the night there. They searched my bookbag and found some razor blades, which they took. "Just a precaution," they said.

I told them, "I'm not suicidal any more and I'm not crazy. You don't need to keep me here."

They said, "We're trained to view things in a disease model. People just don't present the way you were presenting and report what you are reporting if there's nothing wrong."

They asked lots of questions like "What does it mean when we say a rolling stone gathers no moss? That people who live in glass houses shouldn't throw stones? What day is this? Where are you? Who's the President of the United States? How far is it from New York to Paris?" I answered them all, except how far it was from

New York to Paris, and I guessed at that. They wrote everything down.

I spent the night. The next morning I told them I had to leave to go to classes, and they said I would have to sign something and could only leave 72 hours after signing it. That would take up the whole weekend. I signed the paper, and that afternoon a deputy sheriff came and read papers to me which said I had been involuntarily committed to a mental facility. I would have to stay for at least 10 days.

I was furious. I blamed "that thing" for getting me in trouble. "That thing" told me *from this point on your only job is to get out of here. Say whatever you have to say and do whatever you have to do, but you have to get out of here. Remember what I say.* Then it looked at me as if it had Down's syndrome and disappeared. (By the way, when it showed me its face, it was always my face. This time it was what my face might look like if I had Down's syndrome.)

I never heard from "that thing" again.

I talked to a psychiatrist. I heard her thinking *boy, we've got a live one now.* While I was talking with her, I wondered what she was going to tell me. *I'm going to tell you you're schizophrenic,* she thought. *What else could I tell you? We're certainly not going to admit you're telepathic.*

When I finished telling my tale, I asked her what she thought.

"I'm not sure yet," she said. "It may be bipolar disorder, which can be easily medicated. It may, on the other hand, be a schizoaffective disorder, in which case the prognosis is not very good. I'm going to recommend that you stay here for at least four weeks, so we can try different medications."

I was horrified. "Why can't you just give me the medication and let me go?" I asked.

She told me that the psychotropic medications they had in mind might have unpredictable side effects, and I needed to stay in a hospital setting so my progress could be closely monitored.

I wanted no part of medication that would require that I be

closely monitored. I insisted that I was not really mentally ill, and asked what mental illness could be caused by singing too hard.

"Your belief that singing caused your illness is part of what worries me," she said. "It is impossible that singing would cause delusions and hallucinations such as those which you describe, and your belief to the contrary is just another delusion."

I knew within reason that my singing too hard had been what caused whatever it was that was bothering me, both because of the timing of the appearance of the problem and because of the shooting pains in my diaphragm and head which still continued. Those sharp pains convinced me that my singing had been more dangerous to me than she was giving it credit for being, and from that time on I was convinced that she was wrong about me. In fact, I thought she might be consciously lying to me, if I could believe what I heard her thinking.

They gave me a battery of psychological tests. On one, they showed me pictures of inkblots and told me to tell them what the inkblots looked like. I gave my best guess to each one, but they kept prodding me to see more than I actually saw. "Many people see more than one thing. Tell me what else you see," they would say. I would start making things up, and wondered how they were going to get an accurate view of me if they wouldn't let me answer the way I wanted to.

On another test, they showed me pictures and told me to make up a story to go with each picture. "The story should have a beginning, a middle, and an end," they said. Invariably the picture was a black-and-white image of something that looked really depressing. It would be somebody crying, or a man with a fighting gleam in his eye with a woman restraining him, or a sad young man being consoled by an older man, or something like that. By the time I finished taking that test I was depressed.

Then they gave me the Minnesota Multiphasic Personality Inventory (MMPI). It consisted of hundreds of true/false questions like, "I feel like killing myself" or "I sometimes have the urge to steal things I have no use for" or "I hear the voice of God" or "Sometimes I feel like smashing things." It went on forever like that. I was about at the end of my rope by the time I finished taking it. I believe there was even a question that asked whether I heard things that no one else could hear, and to me, that was the crux of the whole problem. If other people could hear the things I heard, then I was telepathic. Otherwise, maybe these doctors were telling me the truth, and I was really mentally ill. I just didn't know which was the case, but it seemed to me that everyone else could hear the same things I could, judging again from their body language. It all seemed to fit so neatly.

Every morning they woke me up early and took my temperature and blood pressure. I didn't see any purpose in that, but I let them do it. Then they served breakfast, which wasn't very good and which I didn't have to eat, but I did have to stay out of bed until it was over. Then I went back to my room and slept until lunch. I had told everything I could think of about being telepathic, and now I decided that "that thing" was right and my number one priority should be getting myself out of this mess and back into law school where I belonged.

The doctors had other ideas, though. They recommended that I drop out of law school. That I was not willing to do, especially since I had already signed a one-year lease on an expensive apartment, had taken out student loans to pay for it, and besides didn't want a one-year delay in my law education. My mother came to see me as soon as she learned where I was, and we talked about my reasons for being there at some length. I didn't tell her the whole truth, though, because I was already planning to get out as soon as possible, and if these people were going to tell me I was crazy for telling the truth, then I just wouldn't tell the truth any more. They had power over me because they had keys to the ward and I didn't, and that was something I didn't like at all.

I started telling everyone that the whole telepathy story had just been my imagination, a product of some unfortunate coincidences that made me think other people knew my thoughts. I faked my way through the psychological tests they gave me, and every minute of every day I acted as normally as possible. I had my mother go to my locker over at the law school and get my books so I could study and not fall too far behind my classmates. On the weekends I watched football on television, and tried to get to know some of my fellow patients, many of whom had been in and out of places like this all their lives. I was the only one I met who was refusing medication.

Outside my window the early October weather was simply gorgeous, and I was missing it.

Finally the day of my hearing before a magistrate came. I could hear everything people were thinking in the courtroom. The judge thought *I know that's you.* I wondered what he was going to do, and he thought *we'll just have to wait and see.*

The state put on its case first. A number of doctors testified as to the things I had told them, and they told the judge that I was "subject to psychotic thought processes." My psychiatrist told the court that I had "reconstituted" during my time in the hospital, which showed that I needed a structured environment away from the pressures of law school in which to recuperate. I thought that was absolute nonsense, because my time in the hospital had only made the pressures of law school that much worse on me, since I was falling behind during my all-important first year. Being in the hospital hadn't magically made all of that go away, as she was suggesting. I knew I had "reconstituted" because I could act like there was nothing wrong any time I wanted to, which I believed I could do because I thought I wasn't really mentally ill. I was likewise faking it now because I wanted out of that hospital she seemed to think was having such a therapeutic effect.

When it was my turn to testify, I told the court that my having become upset on campus was simply a result of some unfortunate coincidences which had led me to believe others knew more about what was going on in my mind than they actually did, and that my claims to being telepathic were therefore just a product of my imagination. I didn't think I was perjuring myself any worse than the doctors had in not admitting before the court that I was telepathic, and besides "that thing" really did seem to be gone for good. *Heck,* I thought. *Maybe it really was just my imagination.* The judge paid very close attention to my demeanor while I was testifying, and when I was finished he made his ruling. He found that I was "subject to psychotic thought processes," but that he was going to release me. I was elated.

That was on a Friday, and my parents and I decided to take the weekend off and go to the beach together. While we were there, they questioned me closely about my "psychotic thought processes," with the idea of having me medicated. I insisted that nothing was really wrong, and that the "unfortunate coincidences" story was the truth. I did this because I thought they were lying to me. I could hear them thinking that they were going to tell me I was mentally ill when I was in fact telepathic, and would continue to hound me about it if I ever brought the subject up again. I didn't bring it up when they didn't, and we had a good time together at the beach.

Finally I returned to classes. I was embarrassed by the whole hitting-myself-and-crying episode, but none of the students was insensitive enough to mention it. My Contracts professor thought *just paint by the numbers from now on and they'll forget about it.* That was exactly what I planned to do.

It was difficult, though. I might be studying in the law library at night and hear men thinking things like *I like to fuck little girls. I like to hurt them and hear them cry out when I get off.*

While I was hearing this I would hear little girls somewhere thinking *Daddy's hurting me! Make him stop!* It was very disturbing, especially since I considered children to be my friends.

It's your wheelchair birthday, I would hear grown women thinking. I had no idea what that meant, but I knew I wasn't supposed to like it.

I worked as hard as I could anyway, trying to shut those things out of my mind, but they would always interfere with my concentration. *We're not going to let you do that,* people would think. *We're not going to let you get that law degree.*

Sometimes people would think *we'll make it up to you,* but I knew they were just playing word games with me. They loved playing word games. "We'll make it up to you" just meant they would keep making up nonsense to think toward me, not that they were going to compensate for any of the terrible things they had already done to me, like sending me into a psychiatric ward with the weight of the world on my head. It was really too much. *Terrible,* the women would think. *You're terrible.*

Also, they started calling my telepathy a *telephone. The telephone keeps ringing and ringing off the wall, but I just can't get up to answer it,* women would think. That meant they wouldn't listen to my appeals to openly admit that I was telepathic.

You don't really have this thing. I just thought I would tell you, the women would think, or *this is a new kind of people,* or *the way you went around slapping yourself and screaming, it makes me think there's something not too good about this thing you seem to think you have.*

Yeah, I would think, *well if you know what I "seem to think," then that tells me a lot.*

No, don't help me. You don't really have this thing. I just thought I'd tell you, they would reply.

Of course, sometimes they would think *okay, you're telepathic,* but I needed them to say it out loud, not just think it. Then men would think *you want us to say it in telepathic words of speech and communication.* As always, that was just more nonsense for me to have to listen to. They knew what I really needed.

We'll make it up to you, they would think.

I tried to get as much out of law school as I could under the circumstances anyway. My Civil Procedure professor was a brilliant lecturer, and I would sit in class marveling at his command of the material and his aura of intelligence. I also liked my Contracts professor, who often said funny things like, "The offer-or is always the master or mistress of his or her offer." The thought of a female contracting party being the "mistress of her offer" made me laugh. Both of those professors thought funny things, too.

One day, soon after I returned to school from my trip to the psychiatric unit, I got a note in my mailfile to talk to one of the law school deans. He said he had gotten several complaints from female law students that I had been staring at them in the library. Of course, I had been listening to all the awful things they were thinking, but I couldn't admit that. He knew about my stay in the psychiatric unit, and wanted to know if I had a mental illness that was causing my behavior. I denied it. He gave me a list of other possible reasons for the behavior. One of them was "gross imma-turity." He asked if there were any other reasons I could think of, and I said there weren't. I wasn't about to tell him I was telepath-ic, or that I had a mental illness. He asked which of the reasons applied to me. I don't remember exactly which one I chose, but I think it was "gross immaturity." I would have said anything to get out of there, even if I'd had to say I was a repressed homosexual or something. I left the dean's office thinking that people were really playing hardball with me now. That really took the cake, to think all those awful things at me and then complain that I was staring at them while they did it!

Then I had second thoughts. Maybe I should have told the dean that I was going crazy, or maybe I should have stuck to my guns and insisted I was telepathic. While I was wondering what to do, I took stock of the situation to establish what I knew for cer-tain so that I could guess at the rest. Of one thing I was sure—something was thinking inside my mind, and it wasn't me! None of my thoughts were secret anymore. Whatever it was, it knew everything I knew, but it processed that information differently from me. Whether it was other people who knew what I was thinking, I didn't know, but someone (or something) definitely did.

It would say things I didn't expect. For instance, one day I was sitting in my Contracts class and we were studying installment contracts under the Uniform Commercial Code. The casebook presented an illustration in which loads of firewood were being sold on an installment basis. The professor called on me to apply the relevant law to the problem, and in my answers I was required to say the words "load" and "firewood" several times. When I successfully got through the grilling I heard a little female-sounding thought in my head say *you fired a load*.

That was pretty typical of the kind of stuff I would hear, something dirty or sexual. It was utterly beyond my control.

November of 1992 passed much the same way. I had irrevocably gone on record (and out on a limb) saying I was telepathic, so I figured people had better start admitting the truth soon. *You may think you're that thing*, people would think. *Well, I just thought I'd tell you, you probably are.*

With November came the fall elections. I voted for Bill Clinton for president, because he had the guts to advocate bombing the Bosnian Serbs to stop the war. I didn't care that he was a draft dodger as long as he had the right solution to the problems at hand. I also voted for the judge who had released me from the mental hospital, and for Orange County District Attorney I voted for the incumbent, a man named Carl Fox. I didn't know it then, but I was voting for the man who would try to have me executed for murder three years later.

In November of 1992 I was still mad about the Sugar Bear and Candy Bear story, and wondered how people could have had sex with each other through my mental telepathy. *It felt so good when he came in my pussy*, the women would think. *Thank you for everything.*

You didn't even use birth control? I wondered.

No, that thing said not to waste it. It said it would be good for us.

And you don't think you got pregnant?
That thing said we wouldn't get pregnant, they replied.
And you believed it?
We believed everything it said. It had such a good way of saying things.

The more I thought about this, the more I began to suspect that there was about to be a gigantic rash of unwanted pregnancies, more than the abortion clinics were equipped to handle at one time, if every woman I ran across had in fact had the experiences they were telepathically describing. I asked my mother over the telephone how long it took a woman to begin to show if she was pregnant, and she said about five months, sometimes more, sometimes less.

Five months from September would be February, so I thought I had until then to be an unacknowledged telepath. Once all the women began to show that they were pregnant, all hell would break loose, and they wouldn't be able to say they hadn't been warned. I had told everything about it when I was on the mental ward. It would be a catastrophe of Biblical proportions, and it was all because of me and my supposedly nonexistent telepathic gift. *You will see!* I thought. *You will see!*

I need that vibrator, came the reply.

I remember one horrible thing began to happen in November. Now, instead of merely insulting me or causing me to smell strange odors when I thought something people didn't seem to like, they began to mess with my left shoulder. That was the shoulder I had dislocated when I was in high school, the one that I had to have surgery on and that prevented me for medical reasons from joining the Army when I had wanted to. *I'm your doctor,* a female thought would say, and then give the bone a tug against the socket. It was both painful and alarming. The shoulder had been fine since the operation, and I was able to do at least 50 pushups at a time on it, plus 10 or more pullups, but now all of that abruptly came to a stop. I would have days when I had to hold my left arm tightly against my side to keep those alien thoughts from pulling the bone out of the socket. I would sit in class, still focused as always on the M-1 rifle to keep the vibrator away, and the shoulder would begin to twitch uncontrollably. I even had to stop playing my bass guitar so much because it required that I extend my left arm, and I had to quit my new band without our ever having played a single gig.

How could this be a mental illness? I wondered. I had never heard of a mental illness that caused such severe physical pain. I couldn't wait for all those babies to be born so I would have lots of little allies in this hostile world. I say "lots of little allies" because children never seemed hostile to me, and babies were the best of all. They seemed so open-minded about me in what they would think toward me that I came to love all children for their minds, which is something I wouldn't have been able to say before that fateful night at the Sig Ep house.

With December came final exams, and I was getting very stressed out. I was woefully unprepared. Despite my best efforts, ever since my trip to the mental ward I had only fallen farther and farther behind. Finally one day I was sitting in a fast-food restaurant and a little boy thought *why don't you just take your exams cold? Don't study. Just write what you already know.*

I thought this over and decided it was a good idea. As usual, a child had saved the day. With an epidemic of unplanned pregnancies looming on the horizon, who had time to worry about silly old law school? I decided to go to a bar and have a good time getting drunk instead, so that's what I did.

Just take 'em cold, the boy thought as I was leaving, obviously pleased with himself for having such a good idea.

At around the same time of year I was in Linda's Bar and Grill having a beer one night, and I saw some young women drinking mixed drinks. *Don't you know you shouldn't drink when you're pregnant?* I wondered toward them.

I know that's you, they thought. They were obviously having a good time.

I got mad. "Don't you know you shouldn't drink when you're pregnant?" I asked one of them.

"I'm not pregnant," she said.

"Yes you are," I said. We argued about it, and she complained to the bartender, who happened to be a friend of mine. He was John, a former housemate of Roger, my former drummer. John kicked me out of the bar. I eventually forgot about the incident, and didn't think of it again until John testified about it at my murder trial.

I took my exams without studying and just wrote what I thought the law was on each problem, then applied it to the facts. I felt like I would pass, but not much more. Then I went back to the mountains for the holidays.

As always, drivers in the cars on the interstate would communicate telepathically with me all the way home, and by the time I got there nothing had changed in my relationship to other people. They were playing just as dirty as ever. I tried to act like nothing was wrong whenever I was around my parents because I didn't want them to force me onto medication I wasn't sure I needed. After all, if I was really telepathic, why medicate the phenomenon? It was a gift, not an illness. I just had to get other people to admit what was going on, and then it would surely be to my benefit. I thought it would just be a matter of a few months before all the women turned up pregnant, and then people would have to admit I had been right all along. It would be a disaster, to be sure, but not one I had caused. I had done my best to get people to behave reasonably regarding me, but as "that thing" had said, they just wouldn't listen. They had to have things their way. Maybe these monsters deserved what they were about to get, but I certainly didn't appreciate being strapped in for the ride.

On Christmas morning I heard a female thought that said *I got you a shiny new vibrator for Christmas. I hope you hate it.* I clung to the image of the M-1 rifle to keep the image of a shiny new vibrator they hoped I would hate out of my mind.

One night during the holidays I saw the old drummer for the Beatles, Ringo Starr, on a late-night talk show. As soon as he came onto the stage he thought *I know that's you, and by the way, that John Lennon you used to go around with wasn't real. It wasn't the John I knew, it was just something you made up.* I thought this might be so, but that it was interesting that Ringo Starr even knew that the image of John Lennon had used to "go around" with me. Or was I just going crazy?

During this time I was terribly lonely for female companionship. I was tired of hearing so much telepathic sexual innuendo while being left out. I didn't trust any women, given what I had heard them thinking all that time, but I decided that was something I was going to have to overcome. It simply wasn't natural for a man to go through life like that. Therefore, my New Year's resolution for 1993 was to ignore as best I could what I heard women thinking and try to find something about them to love anyway.

I returned to Chapel Hill in January and discovered that grades for the previous semester had been posted. I got two Cs and three Ds. One more performance like that and I would flunk out. I didn't worry about it too much, though, thinking that if all was right then by the next round of exams the female classmates of mine would all be very pregnant by men they didn't really love. It made my own troubles seem minor.

One day I was in a supermarket buying groceries and I noticed the Time magazine cover for that week. It showed two weeping Bosnian women who looked like a mother and daughter. The title of the cover article was "A Pattern of Rape." I bought the magazine, took it home, and read it. It was very disturbing, and served to further convince me that American military intervention would be necessary to stop the war before such atrocities became even more common. It also made me wonder if this was the first tangible sign of the deviant sexual behavior of others I had perceived and described to the doctors at the mental hospital. It certainly had a lot in common—the systematic rape of female civilians in Bosnia by soldiers had reportedly begun at exactly the time I started getting my vibrator under control, and included girls as young as six years of age, which reminded me even more of what I had been hearing. I was horrified to see my worst nightmares coming true, and would have done anything to have prevented it, or stop it before it went any further.

On January 23 I went to a bar to hear what people were thinking. There I met an old friend who introduced me to a pretty girl, whom I will call Annetta. I thought she was probably pregnant, and I was having to concentrate so hard on my M-1 rifle that it was hard to think of things to say to her, but we hit it off anyway. I got her telephone number and called her a few days later to ask her out. We began dating, and by February we were starting to fall in love with each other. Not only was she pretty, but I also found her intelligent and gifted with a wonderful sense of humor, which kept my spirits up in these dark times. At first I thought I might even bite the bullet and help her raise the child she was probably bearing, but as the weeks wore on it became apparent that neither she nor many other women were suddenly turning up pregnant. *That thing said we wouldn't get pregnant,* they thought. *I told you what it said. We didn't really do anything except in our minds, but I belong to these other men now.*

I was devastated. It looked more and more like this was just a mental illness, and now my law school career was in serious jeopardy. I didn't tell Annetta about what was really going on because I was trying to make a favorable impression and I was afraid it would scare her away. Besides, there were more pleasant things to say and do. We went to several weddings of friends during February, both her friends and mine, and talked about what it would be like to get married. I was beginning to think of marrying Annetta.

During this time I was still singing along with tapes whenever I got the chance, straining myself in an effort to duplicate what I heard and thus become as good a singer as the best. Annetta asked me not to do it when she was around. She said it got on her nerves, so I stopped altogether. After a few weeks of not singing my head began to feel better and the hallucinations, since that's what I was beginning to think they were, became both less frequent and less severe. So that was it! I now dared to hope that I finally had the problem licked.

Annetta and I began studying together. I worked very hard to make up for lost ground, and fortunately was now better able to concentrate because the hallucinations weren't bothering me as much. March came and went, and things were looking better.

Then came April. One balmy spring night Annetta and I were drinking beer together on the outdoor patio of a local bar, and she said one of her friends knew another law student who said I'd had a nervous breakdown in September. "What happened?" Annetta wanted to know.

"I'd rather not say," I replied.

She kept at it, and I resisted telling her anything about it. I desperately wanted not to have to open that whole can of worms now that things were improving because, as before, I was afraid Annetta would be scared away from me if she knew the truth. Finally I admitted that the doctors believed I had some form of mental illness, but that things were much better now, so there was nothing to worry about.

She seemed satisfied with that. "I was worried it was over a girl," she said.

Exam time came again. This time I hadn't fallen behind, though, and felt far better prepared than I had been in the fall. I studied hard, answered the questions to the best of my ability, and earned three Bs and two Cs. That was better than a full letter-grade higher than my performance the previous semester, and gave me a C average overall, which was good enough to keep me in school. This time there were actually some students who didn't do as well as I did, in spite of all my problems. I felt sorry for them.

In all my efforts to study well enough to keep from flunking out, I hadn't bothered to line up a summer job, so I enrolled in summer school to boost my grade point average. I took the full load of two courses, worked hard, and got Bs in both of them. One of those courses was Environmental Law, and I found it so interesting that I was considering becoming an environmental lawyer. To reward myself for my progress I took the rest of the summer off and returned to the mountains without Annetta.

In her absence, and with some spare time on my hands, I undertook to work on my singing voice again. There was a song by Aerosmith, "Back in the Saddle," which I had thought for a long time would be a real crowd-pleaser if it could be done properly, so I focused on it. Aerosmith's lead singer Steven Tyler was really belting out the high notes on that one, and I tried to imitate his abilities. I never quite got his range, but I sure did scream a lot in trying, and after a couple of weeks the sharp pains in my right side and in the right side of my head began again, and with them came the hallucinations in their former intensity. My left shoulder again started to levitate painfully when I tried to think. *Don't sing*, I often heard people thinking.

All of this just served to convince me that it was my singing that was causing the whole thing. A month before all those problems, though not completely absent, were nevertheless nowhere near as severe as they had now become. I thought the doctors who had told me I was delusional for thinking singing had caused it were completely wrong, and that served to undermine my confidence in everything else they had told me. It even occurred to me that by singing so hard I had begun a process that had yet to become completed. I thought that maybe I could complete the process only by singing harder still, so that I could finish the injury, cross that last threshold, and become accepted as being completely telepathic. Perhaps only then would people stop being so senseless and cruel about it.

At the end of July Annetta came to the mountains to be with me for a few weeks before school started again. At first I didn't mention anything about the renewed hallucinations (if that was what they really were, which I was beginning to doubt), because I thought either they really were just hallucinations, in which case it might be best to keep my mouth shut to keep from scaring her away, or I was telepathic, in which case she couldn't be trusted to tell me the truth. While I was making up my mind, I once again just acted like nothing was wrong, concentrated on keeping the M-1 rifle in and the vibrator out, and tried to make the best of it. In any event I was glad to be with her again.

In August we returned to Chapel Hill. Everyone on the streets seemed to be thinking things at me, and before long I found myself leaning toward believing I was a genuine telepath, and not mentally ill. I started spending more time in bars again so I could be around people to hear what they were thinking. The pregnancies debacle seemed long ago now, and I thought surely all the sexual stuff I had heard had really just been in their minds, and never actually physically consummated. At least that's the general drift I got from them now, and I was willing to believe it.

One day Annetta and I took a hike at Jordan Lake a few miles outside town. While we were there I told her about my belief that singing had caused me to become telepathic. She questioned me about this belief, and suggested that I begin taking medication for the problem. I said that it was a problem only because people insisted on abusing my gift without admitting what they were doing, and that if they would only play fair, then my telepathy was not something I would want to take medication for. It simply wouldn't be appropriate, because this wasn't a true mental illness. Annetta persisted, and got upset when I refused to even hear of seeing a doctor. "I thought you said it was all over with and that you were better now," she said.

"I was until I tried singing all those high notes," I said. "That was what made it worse, and I've never heard of a mental illness that was caused by singing too hard. This is something different, something new."

"No it's not. Wendell, I think you've got a mental illness that's ruining our lives as long as you don't do anything about it."

"It's not a mental illness," I said, and wouldn't listen to her arguments. She later told me it was the worst day of her life.

It all seemed so real. People would think things at me that I myself could never have thought of, and I tried to discover how it all worked so I could understand it and deal with it better. One night I was thinking back over how it had all unfolded, and when I got to the vibrator part I heard now-President Bill Clinton think *and then you put your foot down.* We conversed telepathically for a while, and I found him unlike anyone else I had run across in this strange new world. For one thing, he alone seemed impressed with my feat of replacing the vibrator with the M-1 rifle in my mind, and besides that he seemed to think my original vibrator predicament was funny to begin with.

As our silent conversation continued, I found him to be one of the brightest people I had run across, and also one of the most fun. He was always joking around with me, and his jokes were remarkably witty. He seemed to understand the telepathic environment better than I did, and made use of its idiosyncrasies to come up with some very clever remarks. As always, he displayed insights I would never have thought of, and over time he became the person I would prefer to be with over anyone else in the world except Annetta, because of his obvious brilliance and helpfulness in assisting me to see myself in a more favorable light.

For example, he called my vibrator a *brater.* I found that to be less offensive than "vibrator," which sounded like a dildo. From then on, whenever I communicated with Bill Clinton his words were always studded with *brater* this and *brater* that. It got pretty amusing at times.

Over the next few days and weeks people would think *he talks to Presidents* at me. A few times I thought I even heard them say out loud the phrase, "talks to Presidents." Catching comments like that just served to cement my belief that this was something that existed outside my own mind, involving theirs as well. In other words, it just helped convince me that I really was telepathic, and I thought it was reasonable to believe that. The hard evidence seemed to justify such a belief.

People's ability to alter a phrase to serve their own ends was remarkable, and any phrase that had ever stuck in my mind was fair game. For example, when I was an undergraduate I had studied a poet from the First World War who wrote the words, "My medals? Ripped from my back in scarlet shreds. That's for your poetry book." Later, before my band chose to call itself "Tequila Mockingbird," the guitar player jokingly suggested that we call ourselves "Pagan Daydream." Now, years after these phrases had passed from my conscious memory, a law student in one of my Fall 1993 classes was thinking about how he and the rest of my classmates had twisted my telepathic gift to satisfy their own perverted ends, and thought *I'm eating me. That's for your cloven daydream.* Things like that always threw me, and I almost burst out laughing right there in the middle of the lecture. "Cloven daydream," indeed.

One hot day in September I was walking back from class, struggling with all the interference with my thinking that people seemed to be intentionally creating. I called this being "brainpanned" because it felt like my brain was being pushed down into the bone underneath it from all the singing pressure. Just then an old man stopped me on a street corner. "Excuse me," he said, "is there a telepath around here?"

I was stunned. After all this time for someone to actually say it was almost unimaginable. Had I heard him correctly? "I'm sorry," I said. "What did you say?"

"I mean a bicycle path," he said. "Is there a bicycle path around here?"

"Oh, I don't know."

"Oh, okay. I'm sorry to bother you," he said apologetically, and we both went our separate ways. The incident really stuck with me, partly because I was almost certain I had heard him correctly the first time, and partly because he didn't have a bicycle and he looked too old to be riding one anyway. I have often since wondered about the exchange, and long after it was too late I realized that he might have heard me on one of the days that I had gone around openly proclaiming myself to be the first genuine telepath, and he had remembered me. It's the only explanation that I now feel comfortable with, but at the time I took it as further concrete evidence that I was indeed telepathic, and that I could therefore take stock in everything I perceived.

Also in the fall of 1993 people began thinking a new word, "segue" (pronounced "segway"). I didn't know what it meant, but they kept using it. They would think something like *that was a good segue* when I responded alertly to their nonsense. I had to look the word up, and it means "one thought leading directly into another." I never knew that before I looked it up, but in that light people's use of the word made sense. I took this as another sign that I was in fact telepathic and not mentally ill, because there is no way my own mind could have come up with so many accurate uses for the word before I even knew what it meant. Other people must be doing this, I reasoned.

Of course I'm doing it, they thought. A female thought added *I mean to have you for my very own, over to my place, for dinner.* This sounded sinister to me because I knew, in the way only a telepath can know, what they really meant: that I was to be the main course. A moment later they agreed. *I want to cook you and eat you,* they thought.

That spider on the wall, women would think. *Make it stop looking at me.* By that I took them to mean that I was the "spider on the wall," and that they wanted me to stop hearing their thoughts.

Sometimes I would find myself in a situation like standing in an elevator with someone, and they would think *man, this is making me nervous. Here I am standing right next to this thing.*

One thing I had discovered that was fun to do was go to bars on football Saturdays and drink beer while watching UNC football games with all the other fans there in Chapel Hill, and listen to what everyone, including the players on television, was thinking. I really got into the games that way. There was no telling what a player would think as the game progressed, or what a fan there in the bar would think toward him or me or another fan in response. It got really intense at times, but people usually went away happy because it was a good season for Tar Heel football. I know I had fun, and I kind of miss all that excitement, with the added dimension of entertainment afforded by my apparent telepathic abilities, now that all of that is no longer available to me.

One day that semester I was walking across campus on my way to class and someone handed me a religious pamphlet with a picture of Israeli Prime Minister Yitzhak Rabin and his former nemesis, Yasser Arafat of the PLO, shaking hands over the historic peace agreement they had signed earlier that year. Behind them stood my good buddy, Bill Clinton. The pamphlet proclaimed that this peace agreement between Jews and Arabs was the fulfillment of a Biblical prophecy, and that the Second Coming of Christ and the end of the world were imminent.

As I walked away, people started thinking things like *you're Jesus. You're the one. People know you all over the world. Please don't hurt us for what we did to you. We knew it was wrong, but we did it anyway. Please don't hurt us.* I wasn't so much worried that I was really Jesus Christ as I was that people would think I was and treat me accordingly, like they thought it was the end of the world and they could do anything they wanted because it was all foreordained anyway.

I'm glad I was here to see it happen, thought one man. *I liked that part the best, where I got your little honey and made her do things she didn't want to do. It makes me feel good to know I was a part of it, and kept you from getting anything you wanted. Please don't hurt us.* People kept up this kind of talk from then on from time to time, and it got kind of scary thinking what they had the power to do if they all decided it was what they wanted. After all, the human race did have in its power the ability to exterminate itself if it so chose, and there were times that I suspected that was where we were all headed. After all, hadn't people thought they would wait until 2000, and then BOOM? This worry was to plague me for the rest of the time I thought I was a telepath.

October passed into November, and gradually something I had noticed occasionally before became more and more frequent. Now, instead of merely thinking nonsense words and phrases at me, people were actually saying those same phrases out loud. I would go somewhere, and all of a sudden people would start saying things like "good attitude" or "I know that's you" or "don't hurt me anymore." I would think things at them, and someone from across the room would blurt out an answer to what I had thought. People were dropping names of my family members and mentioning things about my personal life and thoughts that they had no way of knowing without having been told.

And they would laugh. I took it personally. It really seemed like they were intentionally making fun of me, as if they knew there was nothing I could do. After all, what could one man do against the whole world, when they were all in on the joke together and could just tell him he was crazy when he tried to assert himself? It was a terribly lonely feeling, and it seemed to have no end.

I heard people in bars say "Supreme Court" whenever I tried to silently appeal to their sense of justice. They would say "Beatles" when I thought about how this had all come about, or thought of something good. They would say "we did that too well" when I thought of my powerlessness. When I tried to have courage, they would say "Bastogne," which is where my father was wounded in the leg by shrapnel during World War II, or they would say "Purple Heart" when I thought of how I was being hurt by their cruelty. These were just isolated words and phrases they would blurt out, not part of legitimate sentences or conversations. When I confronted them, they would deny having said what I clearly and distinctly heard. It was absolutely maddening.

With December came exams. I was becoming a better law student as time went on, and though I had spent less time studying this semester than I had in the spring, I had spent the time I had studied learning the most important things, so I felt ready. I took the exams and then Annetta and I went to the mountains together for a few days. On Christmas day we went to a town in the North Carolina Piedmont to be with part of her family, and then drove to her mother's and stepfather's home in the Sandhills region that night. For a Christmas present she gave me the new Nirvana album just out that year, "In Utero." I loved it.

A few days later we returned to Chapel Hill and spent New Year's Eve at a party there together. The next day the Tar Heels were to play Alabama in the Gator Bowl, and I went to a bar as usual to watch the game. Also as usual, people in the bar seemed to be talking about me. A cameraman for a local news station came to the bar to film the fans watching the game, but even while he was filming, everyone just kept saying things like "Fonda" (my mother's name), or "Supreme Court," or "Beatles" or whatever, usually depending on what I was thinking at a given moment. A lot of what I heard them saying had nothing to do with the game. They seemed to be paying more attention to me than they were to what was on the big-screen televisions placed all around the bar, and I supposed the cameraman was catching it all.

"They talk around it," people seemed to be saying out loud through the din of the crowded bar. "Tell him his telephone isn't working. . . that's what they're saying. . . I hope it gets better. . . we can't tell him yet."

That gave me an idea. Why not videotape people making all these off-the-wall comments while I was around, and thus provide hard proof that these strangers knew more about me than I ever could have told them? The more I thought about it over the next couple of weeks, the better I liked the idea. Someone had told me that Duke University maintained a parapsychology lab, and I thought that would be the most appropriate place to take my videotapes once I made them. Thus, with my mother's money, on January 19 I bought a small 8mm camcorder from the local Radio Shack. As soon as I had figured out how to run the thing I started carrying it with me to bars, to classes, to any place people gathered and talked their nonsense about me.

"I'll try not to hold a grudge against him when this comes out," someone might say.

Or someone might say, "It taught us to be with girls. We thought we were in, but we were more in with you. It's very unusual."

You won't win, someone might think, and then they would say out loud, "Listen to how he does it. . . I hate how he does that."

All through February I made these videotapes, planning to edit them down to maybe one hour of the most incriminating evidence. I noticed that people usually were reluctant to talk about me while the camera was running, but still I thought I was getting some good material. People silently called it my *vibrator camera* and asked me to put it away, but just to show what a good sport it was I started thinking of it as my "bratercam" for short, and kept on filming.

All of this was simply too much for Annetta. As soon as she learned what I was using the camcorder for she broke up with me, telling me that I needed help, and not to come around her anymore. She did relent enough to let me keep parking my car in front of her house so I wouldn't have such a long walk to classes, but she said she definitely wasn't interested in dating me.

This didn't really bother me at the time. I was convinced she had betrayed me, was lying to me, trying to convince me that I "needed help" when really it was everyone else who "needed help," that she wouldn't admit the truth, and so on. On the last day we were together I accused her of knowing I was telepathic the whole time, and that I now knew that she had known. She thought *well I guess you know about me and the whole Hill, then, too.* "Whatever," she said. I walked out. We had been together for a year, and it was over.

Meanwhile, I kept filming, and what I was after kept showing up. One young woman I knew, just after I had set the camera up in a bar one evening, sat down beside me and said, "Well, Wendell, you certainly have some interesting medals." I didn't have any medals, at least none she would have known about. The only medals I had were the ones I had occasionally awarded myself for the little successes I had from time to time, just for fun, and only in my mind, like the award for the "heaviest man alive." How could she know about this if I wasn't telepathic?

I rushed home that night with my bratercam to see if it had picked up her comment, but it hadn't. She had cunningly said it too quietly for the microphone to detect.

When I wasn't filming, I was singing along with the Beatles and Nirvana, and especially the new album Annetta had gotten me for Christmas. My favorite song on it was called "Milk It," and contained the verse:

I have my own parasite
I don't need a host to live
We feed off of each other
We can share our endorphins

Bill Clinton broke in one day while I was singing along with this and said *milky endorphins.* I also knew of a Pink Floyd song called "Breast Milky," and Bill Clinton thought that was an awfully funny name for a song. Another day I was drinking coffee with cream and Bill Clinton thought *breath milky.* From then on it was *milky* this and *milky* that.

For most people, though, it was still *Beatles* this and *Beatles* that, or *vibrator* this and *vibrator* that. Bill Clinton thought *it has something to do with their milky endorphins. That's why they think that way.*

Sometimes I would spend a whole night out in my car, parked in an empty church parking lot, drinking beer and singing along with tapes. When I got home just before dawn, the birds would be singing. *Cheer up, cheer up,* they sang. *It'll be all right.*

On Nirvana's song "Dumb," Kurt Cobain sang the words "Soothe the burns/ Wake me up." It sounded exactly like "Soon the birds/ Wake me up," and it made me look forward to these early morning sessions where I lay in my bed, trying to go to sleep while listening to the birds singing their sweet little telepathic thoughts.

One morning I was lying there like that, and Bill Clinton thought *Chip. Their minds are like tiny little computer chips.* He seemed to like the way I talked with birds, and from then on always called them "Chip."

Once I was singing along with the Beatles on the song "Nowhere Man." There's a part of the song where they sing lots of la la la la's, and as I threw myself into that part of the song with drunken joyous abandon, Bill Clinton thought *he's off in la-la land.*

I wondered how much film I would have to make before the people at the Duke parapsychology lab would be forced to take an interest in my case, because I was sure they, as well as everyone else, would be reluctant to admit the full scope of the truth. It was something they already knew at least as well as I did, I thought, but how much of it would they admit? I figured the more evidence I had on videotape, the more they would have to fess up to, so I just kept filming. *All in Duke horse,* people thought, meaning "all in due course." One day a woman on Franklin Street thought *just wait till you see what kind of big thinking they've been doing over at Duke, too.*

That winter I had no less than three winter coats stolen from me while I was filming. I thought people resented me for catching them in the act of lying to me about something so important, and were taking their resentments out on me in a childish way. I had no more coats, so I had to resort to wearing a tattered old Army jacket with the words "Dr. Feelgood" stenciled on the back. It was the only thing I had, and I thought it was so ugly that no one would want to steal it.

One night I was at Don's apartment and I was thinking about how profound it was that every man, woman, and child on the planet knew all about every thought that had ever passed through my mind, and Don thought *yeah, we all know about you and your national vibrator.* I couldn't help but laugh. "National vibrator," indeed. It sounded like some corporation whose legal problems I would have studied in law school, like "Williamson vs. National Vibrator, et al." or something.

I thought about how certain imaginary smells came up at telepathically opportune times, and Don thought *yeah, you've got that shit stinking over here, too.* He didn't say anything, though, crafty devil that he was.

When at last I thought I had enough film footage to begin editing down to the best parts, I started reading through the manuals that had come with my vibracam to learn how to do it. The manual read like, "Attach the VHF socket to the UHF socket," or whatever. I was having trouble understanding it with all the interference going through my mind, and suddenly someone I hadn't thought of in a long time thought *socket* at me, like the word had caught his attention. It was Clint McRory, an ex-Marine whose speech I had heard and whose book I had read when I was in junior high school. He had been an outstanding athlete in high school and college, and had quit coaching high school track during the Vietnam War to take an officer's commission in the Marine Corps. He had gone to Vietnam as the leader of an elite recon team, and one night in 1968 his 13-man team's position had been overrun by hundreds of North Vietnamese regulars, hurling grenades and tossing explosive satchel charges. Clint had lost an arm and an eye that night, had his legs mangled by grenade fragments, and had nearly died. He survived years of painful rehabilitation to become an Evangelist preacher. I had admired him greatly, but I hadn't thought much about him lately. *You said 'socket,'* he thought. His own eye was missing, and he showed me what it felt like to have an empty socket.

My shoulder was still levitating in its socket beyond my control from time to time, and he thought *you have a socket problem too. Maybe I can help.*

Like Bill Clinton, Clint McRory was to become a shaping force in my life once again, just as he had been in the years when I was considering a military career.

At last I got my 8mm tapes edited down to an hour-long VHF tape, so one day in early March I called Duke University and asked for the number of a parapsychology lab. They told me they no longer had a parapsychology lab affiliated with the University, but that the department had split off and become private. They gave me the private lab's telephone number.

I called it and was answered by a woman with a strong European accent. I explained who I was and what I wanted.

"You're mentally ill," she said. "You need help, and we can't provide it."

I said I had videotapes proving that I was telepathic, but she wasn't interested in even seeing them. I was really put off by her closed-minded attitude, and hung up the phone in frustration. I was really mad.

The next morning I took my tape to class with me, and in the minutes before my Criminal Procedure class began I stood up and announced that I was telepathic, that everyone had been lying to me, and that I had a videotape to prove it. At first everyone just ignored me, which made me even more angry, but then my friend Bill went and got the Associate Dean of Students. The Dean asked me to come with him, but I refused, stating that I had as much right to attend class as anyone else. He made me promise not to disrupt the class, which I promised, and then he told me to come to his office as soon as the lecture ended. I agreed.

After class I went to the Dean's office armed with my video-tape. I explained the situation to him, and asked if he was interested in viewing the tape. He agreed, with the condition that I agree to seek medical help if he wasn't convinced I was telepathic judging from the contents of the tape. Otherwise, he said, the law school would have trouble recommending me for admission to the bar the following year, owing to my unconventional beliefs. I agreed.

We watched the tape together, and I pointed out the places where I thought people were talking about me. I especially heard them say the word "Beatles" a number of times, and not as part of any conversation. They just blurted out the word.

The Dean of Students watched for a while, asking questions. Then he said he found the tape "inconclusive," and that I should therefore accompany him to Student Health, as I had agreed, so we went.

When we got there we were met by a pair of female doctors who seemed worried that I suffered from a seizure disorder that prevented me from controlling my actions. I knew that was just more nonsense, but since The Dean was there I answered their questions politely. They refused to look at my videotape. They made an appointment for me to see one Dr. Myron Liptzin, and The Dean of Students said he would keep up with whether I made the appointment or not. I agreed to go.

At the appointed time I went to Student Health to meet with Dr. Liptzin. He was friendly, and listened attentively as I described my experiences. He reached into his desk drawer and took out a bottle of prescription pills. He said it was a psychotropic medication called Navane, and told me to take one pill a day for the next week, and then to come and see him again. I took the pills with me, and did as he directed. Within a few days I noticed no difference except that it was more difficult to wake up in the mornings.

After several weeks of reporting this to Dr. Liptzin once a week, he lowered the dosage but told me to keep taking the medication.

During these sessions I told him more and more about my beliefs and experiences. I told him about my first visit to Student Health when they had told me I needed an appointment which I didn't make, and he seemed to think their arrangements had been regrettably deficient on that occasion. However, he seemed amused when I said I heard the birds talking to me, and what they said. I described my new shoulder problem, and he said he could get me an appointment at Sports Medicine to develop an exercise program which might help. I declined, because I was sure that until those unseen forces that were tearing my shoulder apart were dealt with, exercise would only make the problem worse. The less I moved that shoulder, the better, and I told him so.

Dr. Liptzin was also the first person I ever told about my vibrator.

"We all experiment sexually," he said. "It's nothing to feel guilty or ashamed about."

"Yeah, well I personally don't feel guilty or ashamed about it," I said, "but other people seem to have a serious problem with it."

He told me other people knew nothing about it, and that my belief to the contrary was just a paranoid delusion which the medication was designed to alleviate. I kept taking the medication all through March.

Then, on the evening of April 6, I was sitting in the Chapel Hill McDonalds eating a cheeseburger, and it suddenly occurred to me that it had been a while since I had heard any alien thoughts, or had to concentrate on my M-1 rifle. I tested around for a bit, and did all the things people always tried to keep me from doing with my thoughts. There was no one there to interfere.

It all came to me at once. I was in fact mentally ill, and needed this Navane to be able to think normally. I was not telepathic at all, and never had been. Everything I had sacrificed to that belief, my law school grades, my girlfriend, my peace of mind, had all been for naught. I had been greatly mistaken.

As soon as I was finished eating, I threw away my trash and went home to get my books. I had planned to spend the evening drinking beer at a bar, listening to what people were thinking, and then spend the rest of the night singing along with my tapes on my car stereo in that empty church parking lot, but now I needed to change my plans, and change them immediately. Exams were less than a month away, and once again I had squandered the best part of the semester trying to get people to admit I was telepathic. There would be no more time for Kurt Cobain this semester.

I closed the library down that night, then went home and went to bed. I studied all day the next day, and the day after that. Then, tired of reading at last, I went to He's Not Here with my law school friend, Bill. We talked there for a while, and I told him about my medication's newfound effects and my great mistake in believing I had been telepathic. Bill said he was glad I was finally coming around, and said he was sure things would work out for me now.

Then he said, "Did you hear about Kurt Cobain?"

"What about him?" I asked.

"He committed suicide today. I just heard about it. Blew his brains out with a shotgun."

We talked about that for a while, and Bill said he was sorry to be the bringer of bad news at such a bad time in my life anyway. I said that was okay, I would have heard about it soon even if he hadn't told me.

That was April 8, 1994.

Later in April I tried to get back in contact with Annetta. I told her I was on medication at last, and that it was working well. I tried to renew our former relationship, but she told me it was too late. She had a new boyfriend, was happy with him, and in fact was upset that I had even contacted her again. She said she had moved on, and that I should do the same. When I told her that

Dr. Liptzin had said he didn't think I was truly schizophrenic or psychotic, she just said, "That doctor had better take a closer look at your record." It was very discouraging.

However, I was able to study well. I continued to see Dr. Liptzin, and reported that my hallucinations were almost entirely gone. Still, from time to time, I heard or saw something that wasn't supposed to be there, but he told me that was probably unavoidable. A higher dose of medication might take care of it, but the increase in side effects could make the situation worse overall. All in all he and I were both pleased with my progress.

I took exams in May. For the third semester in a row, I had no grade lower than a C. All things considered, I thought that was pretty good.

I didn't go to summer school that summer. Instead, I planned to go back to the mountains and study the subjects I had done so poorly in during my first semester of the first year so that I would be better prepared for the bar exam. I told Dr. Liptzin that I was leaving town for the summer, and he gave me a prescription for enough Navane to last two months. During one of these sessions he again told me he didn't believe I was really psychotic or really schizophrenic, but that possibly my past drug use had given me some "sensitive nerve endings" in my brain, which was a condition which might go away over time. He also told me that the medication I was taking did have some unpleasant side effects, and that if at some point in my life I was with someone I trusted, such as Annetta had been, then I could try going off of the medication to see if the hallucinations returned.

As things turned out, that was extremely bad advice.

I returned to the mountains and began reading first-year law subjects I had only peripherally studied the first time through. One day at the beginning of June I took a break and sunbathed all afternoon, forgetting that I had been warned against overexposure to the sun while I was on Navane. I got a really nasty sunburn, and immediately became disenchanted with the medication as a result.

I decided to stop taking Navane at least until the sunburn went away, as my doctor had allowed, and told my parents what I was doing. About two days later I suddenly started feeling physically better than I had felt in months, and that made me want to stay off Navane for good.

I thought that if the symptoms came back I would know them to be an illness, and start taking Navane again. How naive I was.

All through June and July I got along well, studying almost every day, feeling well, and experiencing little or no hallucinatory effect. I thought I was at last back to normal, and without having to take those bothersome pills. I went places with my parents and did what I wanted. They questioned me closely about my decision to go off the medication and how I was doing without it, but I was able to truthfully say that I was having no problem. They seemed skeptical, but I showed no signs of deterioration at that point, and besides that, there really wasn't much they could do.

It was a gradual, almost imperceptible change, but by the time I got back to Chapel Hill in August I was beginning to hear those telepathic messages again.

Hey, Wendell, it's talking to you again, Bill Clinton would think.

You'd better start taking your Navane again, people would think. *I can hear what you're thinking.* Or they would think something like *we liked it when it was quiet around here. Please start taking your Navane again.*

I tried taking my medication, but usually as soon as I put a pill in my mouth the alien thoughts would stop. They didn't even give me time to ingest the pill. I started to wonder if the Navane was correcting the illness, or if people just wanted me to think it was. As I thought about it more, it seemed like people were just trying to convince me I was crazy so they could do as they liked. That way, I would think it was all just me, and they wouldn't have to worry about my trying to make some move to stop them. Admission of this possibility, that the apparent effectiveness of my medication was just a hoax, put me right back to square one as far as discovering the truth was concerned.

That made me boiling mad. *You deserve to die for this,* I thought one day toward those maddening alien thoughts in my head. *You've ruined my life all over again.*

You'd be scared to do it, came the reply. *You'd go to jail.*

I'd blow the cop's head off that tried to take me to jail. I'm pissed off, I thought.

Good attitude, came the answer.

I enrolled in my last year of law school, but the urge to study began to leave me almost immediately. I spent my time in the bars of Chapel Hill, listening to what people thought and wondering what I could do about it. I couldn't expect people to be honest with me, even if I showed them concrete evidence of what was going on. I had learned that much from my experience with the camcorder. All people had to do was deny any knowledge of it, and then suggest that I was mentally ill. If they were going to straighten up, it appeared that they were going to have to be forced. The proof was all around me.

Too many things were happening which I couldn't feel comfortable in attributing to mental illness. For example, what with the pain in my right inner skull and the betrayal of my left shoulder, I began to feel very lopsided. My right side felt much stronger than my left, and in the late summer heat whenever I began to perspire, for every drop of sweat that rolled down my left side, there would be three or four drops of sweat that would roll down my right. That is no exaggeration. One afternoon I was drinking beer at the apartment of a friend named John, and I felt sweat rolling down my right side while my left was completely dry. I told John what was happening, and as I pulled off my shirt to show him, I accidentally knocked over his roommate's glass bong, shattering it into a million pieces. John freaked out, and in the excitement that followed my sweat patterns were forgotten about. Still, it was a genuine phenomenon, just like the shoulder's being willed apart by some consciousness that was not my own. What kind of mental illness could do a thing like that, I wondered, and I decided that it was no mental illness at all. I was being deceived by everyone, I was sure.

In September I began thinking of how I had tried to kill myself two years earlier to keep people from abusing my telepathy. I had been unable to do it then because I believed I had too much going for me, being telepathic and all. I also thought of the concept of "suicide by cop," which I had first heard of in connection with O.J. Simpson's surrender to the police after the famous slow-speed Bronco chase that summer. I wondered if the police would intentionally kill me, knowing they would have to do without my precious telepathy from then on, even if I gave them a reason to kill me. It seemed that this was a classic host/parasite relationship between myself and the rest of adult humanity. Would the parasites kill their host, knowing they couldn't do without him? Even if the host began to kill the parasites?

With that I hit upon an idea that seemed diabolically clever. What if I gave the police a rock-solid reason to kill me, like killing some of them, and they refused to do it? Wouldn't that prove something?

The people around me were listening to me thinking this through and they betrayed some consternation. *You wouldn't do it,* they thought defensively. *You'd be too chicken. We know you, remember? You use that vibrator,* etc. Then they gave my shoulder a painful twinge. *Besides, we wouldn't let you,* they thought. *We'd make sure your shoulder is useless. I'm your doctor, remember?*

Could it be my own mind? I really wasn't sure, but the part with my shoulder made me think it was something more. Also, too many other things had happened to lead me to believe that. What about my aunt talking about her son and his vibrator? What about the man who asked if there was a telepath around there? What about all those times when alien thoughts would catch me off guard and surprise me with something totally unexpected, something I didn't believe my own mind would, or even could, have come up with? What about the isolated words and phrases my vibracam had picked up that made no sense if you assumed people weren't answering my thoughts? What about Kurt Cobain's suicide as soon as the Navane took effect? It was as though he had given up on me. No, there had to be something more to all this than mere "sensitive nerve endings."

I waffled on the question of my medication. Sure, things had improved when I was on it, or at least seemed to. However, if I was really telepathic and these people just stopped interfering with my thoughts when I was on Navane in order to convince me I was mentally ill, then it might be dangerous to medicate myself. Who could say what would happen, if that were the case? What did these people mean when they said they would wait until 2000, and then BOOM? If I were really telepathic, then things like that were reliable information that should be taken into account, and it would then seem that these people posed a real danger not only to me, but to each other as well. Had they scrambled each others' thoughts only to get themselves into a situation no one really wanted? By concealing my brater from myself and others, had I taught others to conceal the truth from themselves too? It seemed that if that were the case, then to go back on medication would be both a cop-out, potentially dangerous to everyone, and also a missed opportunity. I decided if I didn't kill, I would always wonder what would have happened if I had.

Just reach out and take it, people thought. I thought about accepting this challenge, and I also thought about what might happen if I did nothing. I didn't want to misjudge others, and it was my natural inclination not to retaliate even when I was wronged for certain. However, this was different from most other wrongs. In this environment, people couldn't hide the extent of their absolute evil and cruelty.

In my Insurance Law class that semester, the professor was talking about the principle of risk-averseness. Risk-averse people, in essence, prefer a small certain loss to a large uncertain loss. That's why people consider it rational to pay insurance premiums. The small certain loss of the cost of insurance is considered preferable to the large uncertain loss that the insurance policy is bought to cover, even if the large uncertain loss is relatively unlikely ever to occur. People buy insurance knowing that the insurance company takes in more money in premiums than it pays out to cover losses. That's how the companies stay in business, and yet people consider it prudent, even necessary, to keep paying those premiums.

I considered this theory in light of my own dilemma. The large uncertain loss that I wanted to guard against was, quite frankly, the end of the world. I was afraid people might do something crazy because of me. To my knowledge, a telepath had never been seen before. For things to be happening the way they appeared to be, almost no worst-case scenario seemed overly pessimistic, including eventual nuclear holocaust. Nuclear weapons, after all, were controlled by mere humans, and mere humans it seemed were affected by me. Why else would they all, and I mean all, appear so dishonest and mean? It seemed that people had changed in reaction to me. They seemed to be different people from the ones I had known and liked before, and I was now seeing evil in its most powerful and sexual form.

You can't talk to me, they thought.

Of course, nuclear holocaust would be the worst-case scenario, but the end of everything was something people had telepathically alluded to almost ever since the beginning of my experience in this strange new world. All of this was infinitely scarier than the prospect of my own death alone. The stakes couldn't have been any higher.

I was terrified that all the people of the world would react violently against one another when they finally realized what they had been doing to me and to one another. Their efforts would eventually prove false and self-destructive. What would spark this realization was not clear to me, but I suspected that it would be my own death, at which point all of the telepathy would disappear and leave people wondering what had happened. This is a big reason why I didn't just kill myself now. I thought about it. Maybe I couldn't pull the trigger of an M-1 rifle aimed right at my own head, but I could still run a hose from a car tailpipe into the passenger compartment, and consume plenty of alcohol and sleeping pills for good measure. That might give me the escape I needed, but what about the effect it might have on the rest of the world, if I was in fact the host of all these parasites? To be sure, they weren't worth much to me as things stood now, but they once had, and might someday again prove themselves true to me. I didn't want to cause a nuclear holocaust by committing suicide because I couldn't stand the heat of being the world's first and only telepath.

Admittedly, the end of the world was not a certain loss, mostly because I didn't know for certain that I was telepathic and not mentally ill, but I put the probability of the end of the world at somewhere greater than zero. In fact, I put the probability that I was telepathic at about a 50-50 compromise, because for every reason I could think of that I was telepathic, I could think of an equally compelling reason that I was mentally ill, and vice-versa. If I was telepathic and did nothing further to get people to admit it and face the dangers inherent therein, then I put the probability of human self-annihilation at somewhere greater than 50-50, because these people seemed fixed on cruelty, and their boldness was just increasing with time. Thus I put the probability of the end of the world, or something almost as bad, at somewhere between 25% and 50%, which was intolerably high.

We've destroyed ourselves, people thought. *It's not real, is it?*

I felt morally compelled to do something drastic to put a stop to this chain of events that seemed to be unfolding, even if it meant events would prove me wrong in the specifics. I had once taken a logic course as an undergraduate where we learned that the rational decision is not always the right decision. Even if you proceed with a 90% chance of being right, still 10% of the time events will prove you wrong. It can't be helped. The smart money is still with the probabilities, and this new theory of risk averseness threw a new light on the whole question I faced. Somehow I must prove that they were afraid to kill me.

I decided that the risk-averse, and therefore safe, and therefore moral, thing to do would be to kill in order to prove others were afraid to kill me in return, and thus by implication force them to admit that this was because I was telepathic and very important to their scheme of things. The small certain loss I would be paying would be the lives of a number of people, possibly including my own if I was wrong. Almost certainly if I was wrong and survived the shooting part then I would be sent to prison or a mental hospital for a very long time, possibly forever. Still, it was preferable to allowing people to destroy the world, even if the probability that they would do so was relatively small, in this case, less than 50%. To be sure, the lives of a number of innocent people and possibly my own would be a huge price to pay, but that was because the cost of insuring the world against the devil himself was very high. My move would be probably self-sacrificing, but I believed I had the courage to do it, since I was becoming convinced that it would be the risk-averse, safe, and therefore morally right thing to do. Ironically, it appeared to me to be the most compassionate choice. I believed this course of action had a stronger rational and moral basis than any alternative. I wanted them to admit I was telepathic not because I thought I had all the answers, but because I was being wronged, and because we might all be in danger.

Thus went my thinking through September, as the evidence that I was right about being telepathic continued to mount every time I went out in public. If I was crazy, then I was really crazy, because things just kept getting worse and yet more convincing. Still, I had to admit that I might be crazy. Or I might not be. 50-50 either way.

I thought there was a 50-50 chance that my plans were no secret, because people seemed to know all about them without having to be told out loud. They blurted out silly things about it, like they didn't take me seriously, and they laughed a lot. It was infuriating, but I held my anger in check. Let them listen to me make my plans, I thought. Maybe they'll start taking me seriously and I won't have to go through with it after all, if they hear me making good plans for their own deaths.

Now we know you don't want to have to go through with it, they thought. *We knew you'd be too chicken.*

Always there was that question: was it mental illness, or was it a form of mental telepathy so powerful that no one dared admit publicly that it even existed? Was I being paranoid and grandiose, or did I happen to be right on the money? It was a critical decision with life-and-death consequences, and I had to make it correctly. However, no matter how hard I tried to ascertain the truth, I still couldn't be certain either way. Because there was no way I could know what the situation really was, I was forced to make assumptions. I would just have to do my best and be willing to live the rest of my life with the consequences, however it turned out.

My open-mindedness was my undoing. If there was even the slightest chance I was telepathic, then the principal of risk-averseness would kick in and I would be morally compelled to take drastic action to prevent the unthinkable.

I had read once that in 1945, when the U.S. government was developing the atomic bomb, a team of physicists pointed out that there was an infinitesimal chance that the first atomic test would destroy the world. The government ordered a study of the probabilities, and stipulated that if the probability of self-annihilation was above a certain level, then the test would not go forward. The physicists estimated the probability at a lower level, and as we all know the test was performed. I don't remember what the government set as the maximum tolerable level of probability of total annihilation, but it was truly infinitesimal. As I have already said, I placed the probability of the human race's destroying itself because of my telepathy as being low, but not so low as to make continuing on my medication under the assumption no harm would come of it an acceptable course of action. Again, my open-mindedness to the possibilities was the basis for my decision to act.

You won't do it, they all thought.

Oh yes I will, I thought.

You say that now, they answered, *but when the time comes you won't do it. You have too much to lose. You'll keep deciding to put it off.*

They knew me well. It would truly be a terrifying step, and it seemed the more I planned it the less likely it would be that I would have to actually go through with it. People would know about my plans by reading my thoughts, and would know when I was serious. At that time they would surely relent and admit that I had been right all along, which would make killing people unnecessary.

Someone's been poaching in your game preserves, I would hear someone think.

"It's impossible. It can't be happening," I would hear someone say. "I don't like being with you. You're terrible."

Was that something someone would say in normal conversation? I didn't think so, but I was pretty sure I had heard it.

I could tell no one what I was planning, because I wanted them to show that they knew about it without having to be told. That way I might be spared the necessity of bloodshed.

If bloodshed turned out to be necessary, I would have to have lots of ammunition, not only because there were so many people who were wronging me, but more because I wanted to be able to hold out long enough that there could be no doubt that people were afraid to kill me. It would be better to have too much and not use it all than to not have enough and fail because of that. I certainly couldn't afford to be captured alive after I had killed someone but before people had seen that the police were afraid to kill me in return. I decided to wait until January of 1995, so that

I could use my last student financial aid money to buy ammunition. *I won't put it off past the end of January,* I thought toward my detractors. *You've been warned. You'd better straighten up before then.*

I need your vibrator, they thought back. It was infuriating.

"They're not cruel, they're ignorant," someone would say.
"I bet he loses it when we tell him. I'm not telling him."
"He showed me how to use it."
"God must be using him to illustrate a point."
"Even the bottom element will follow him."

All these things I heard, and tried to fathom what I should do about it.

October 1, 1994, was the 50th anniversary of a battle my father's unit had fought in France, at a place called Gramercy Wood. They lost more men on October 1, 1944 than they did on any other day during the entire war except January 4, 1945. At an army reunion in the late 80s, a former platoon sergeant who had been in the battle at Gramercy Wood told me that the men who attacked there were mostly all right, but that the men who tried to escape by going to the rear were killed or wounded by the enemy. Now, 50 years later, I thought it might be the same for me. If I chickened out, then all was lost. If I acted courageously, on the other hand, then maybe everything would work out for me. On that day I decided for sure that I was going to do it, and people had better take that into account in dealing with me. I tried to shut the idea of not doing it completely out of my mind, because if people perceived any hesitance then they would get the notion that I wouldn't really do it, and just keep on the way they were. I would have to be brutal, remorseless, cold-blooded, calculating, from that day forward. There could be no more doubt.

One night I was in Linda's Bar, thinking about military matters with General Schwarzkopf. I was thinking that courage alone does not decide battles. Soldiers with courage get shot down like ducks in a shooting gallery. They need good plans, too.

And pluck, thought Schwarzkopf. He only chose the word "pluck" because I had thought about ducks, and ducks could be plucked. That's an example of the kind of word games some people played with me all the time.

There was a phrase from a book about the Civil War I had read once, and that phrase fell prey to word games. The phrase was "the old 'buck and ball' of army legend," meaning a type of ammunition American soldiers had used before the Civil War. On this night Hillary Clinton, who also conversed telepathically with me sometimes, thought *oh, you just came in here to think about the old buck and bore of army legend.* "Bore" was a funny word to insert, because it could mean "inner rifle barrel" as well as "not interesting." She seemed to have meant both at the same time.

That's a fair wrinkle, thought Bill Clinton. It was a three-way pun. It first made me think of the wrinkles on the brain, like he had just learned something or thought of something he hadn't thought of before. Then it made me think of a wrinkle in the plot. Last, I thought of crow's feet.

The three of us often conversed for hours like that, with thoughts and responses coming quickly and alertly, even after I got too drunk to be very interested anymore. In a way I was trying to escape, in fact, but with little success. The conversations went on whether I wanted them or not. It's hard not to think at all, and it seemed there was always some smart-aleck somewhere who would have a catty response.

I continued to smoke cigarettes in front of these two images of the anti-smoking Clintons, and thought my smoking was insouciant.

It's incessant, Hillary Clinton corrected me.
Don't bother him in his brater madness, Bill thought.
My brater is nobody's brater business but my own, I thought.

Another time I was trying to think how I would be able to look down my nose at these people if I turned out to be right, but they inserted the word *glasses* for "nose," so that what I ended up thinking was *someday I'll really be able to look down my glasses at these people.*

That, I thought, was just an underhanded way for them to remind me that I wore glasses, so I tried thinking the thought again. This time, however, it came out as *someday I'll really be able to look down my nose at these people's spectacles.* I decided that was closer to what I had originally meant, with the added bonus of reminding me that some of them, too, wore glasses.

And maybe we'll all be spared seeing this spectacle you're planning, thought Bill Clinton. I gave up on my first thought and went back to thinking about the spectacle itself.

From the same Civil War book I had gotten "buck and ball of Army legend," I got the phrase "decidedly important if true." It was from a letter a soldier had written lamenting the false impressions given by newspapers of how the war was going. He said they printed falsehoods that would be "decidedly important if true."

I liked the phrase, and used it in my own situation. If these people knew my thoughts as well as it seemed they did, that would be decidedly important if true. A would lead to B would lead to C, until there was a rifle attack by a deeply affronted law student. My telepathy would be decidedly important if true, as would be my mental illness.

When Annetta and I had been together, we had gone with my parents to visit a family in Tennessee who made trolls out of wood, with corn silk hair, acorns for eyes, and so on. These trolls became a real conversation piece in this telepathic environment, and female voices said things like *he likes to play with dolls*, which is what they called the trolls.

And scissors, I added, remembering that scissors had something to do with witchcraft. Trolls, dolls, and scissors. Those were ingredients in my magic, I thought. I thought of myself as a "seer" or a "conjurer," and that my dark art was the most fun to practice when I had been smoking marijuana. Whenever I did, though, General Schwarzkopf would cause me to see a vision of myself in some enchanted garden, stuffing my mouth with forbidden fruit. It was funny. *Put that in your pipe and smoke it,* he would think.

I also went back to trying to imagine my black winged dragon whenever I went out in public, only now it was not to keep the brater away. I had the image of the M-1 to fix that. The dragon was purely for everyone's entertainment. I would picture it crawling around, flying, swimming through stormy ocean waves, scratching and clawing, eating out of garbage dumpsters, and just generally doing whatever it is that dragons do. Of course, I thought everyone else could see it too, and sometimes I would hear comments like "that was good!" or "make it come over here!" from across the room. When I thought people were talking to me out loud, I would often answer them out loud, but when it got too realistic I would get strange looks and be back to fighting against the image of my brater.

Which end are you talking to? Bill Clinton would silently ask when I openly accused people, as if I was talking to the wrong end of a horse or something. Again I would laugh, and again people would stare. I thought they were trying to fake me out by pretending to be baffled at my behavior, so I didn't let their strange looks deter me.

My father had once given me a gold coin, and I started carrying it with me everywhere I went. Whenever something happened that served to convince me I was really telepathic and not mentally ill, I would rub that gold coin. I decided to carry it with me when I finally attacked, as a good-luck charm. I found myself rubbing it often.

I wanted the story of how I had become telepathic to be printed in the newspapers. *Someday you'll be there,* Bill Clinton would think. *Right there on the front page of The Daily Planet.*

One night I was watching a nature program on television at Linda's and they were showing a wolf. My father had told me he once saw an animal that might have been a wolf while he was hiking in the mountains. He said it looked like a big dog with unusually big paws. I looked to see if the wolf on television had unusually big paws, and Hillary Clinton thought *my, what big paws you have.*

All the better to paw you with, thought the wolf.

I was idly wondering what it would be like to paw the first lady, and Bill Clinton thought *yeah, right. In the Lincoln Bedroom, I suppose.*

I answered that there might be poltergeists in the Lincoln Bedroom, and a female thought I said *houseguests.* That was their new word for "poltergeists."

Another night I was thinking about how nice it would be to be in a band which already had a good singer, so that all I would have to do was play bass. *What?* thought Bill Clinton. *And not let us listen to your mule braying?*

I spent so much time thinking about what a catch-22 I was in that I decided to read the novel by Joseph Heller, Catch-22. It turned out to be a war story about insanity, and it had a character named General Scheisskopf. I ribbed General Schwarzkopf a lot about that one. It also had a character named Kraft, who was shot down and killed. One day I was thinking about how I might end up going the same way as Kraft, when suddenly a huge Kraft cheese truck rumbled up Franklin Street near where I was walking. It scared me, showing up like it did at that very moment.

That thought you just had about Kraft, Bill Clinton thought. *It was cheesy.*

That thought you just had about the cheese truck, I thought. *It was too.*

Another funny thing Bill Clinton did was abbreviate the "and" in certain phrases. For example, *stretch the truth and exaggerate* would become *stretch the truth 'n' exaggerate.* The whole situation between myself and the rest of the world became, in his words, a game of *victims and suspects.* If he had already thought that phrase a few times, then it became *victims 'n' suspects.* I found myself playing victims 'n' suspects a lot. The game was about trying to tell who were the victims, and who were the suspects. Was I the victim and the people around me the suspects, or was it the other way around?

Bill Clinton thought of MTV's Beavis and Butthead as *brater suspects.* That seemed about right, I thought.

Very amusing, as though Beavis and Butthead might be suspected of having a few brater secrets of their own.

It seemed no one would stand up for me if I didn't stand up for myself. One day I was eating at a burger place at the local mall, and I noticed a man and what I supposed was his young son come in. *Why won't you help me?* I wondered at the son, because I had more faith in children than I did adults.

You're the one who has to prove it, the boy thought. *There's nothing we can do.*

Oh, I'll prove it all right, I thought. *If that's really what you want. People are going to get hurt, though.*

I can't wait, the boy thought gleefully. *I just can't wait.* He looked directly at me, but maybe that's because I was staring, so I looked away. Then he thought *if you don't believe it's true, why should I?*

Because I might kill your parents, I thought.

Do it, he thought. *I wouldn't mind. They hurt me.*

Good attitude, thought the father. *Is that what you want me to tell you?*

How many times do you have to hear that kind of talk, thought the boy toward me. *And they do it on purpose, too.*

Should I say something out loud? I silently asked the boy.

That wouldn't be too smart, he thought. *My dad's sitting right there.*

Do say something, thought the dad. *Tell us what you're planning to do.*

I couldn't do that, so I paid my bill and left instead, more resolved than ever to settle this thing once and for all.

On Halloween night I went to a law school party, got pretty well intoxicated, and then went in my car to the empty church parking lot I used to sing in so I wouldn't bother anyone. I sat there for hours, drinking beer, singing with all the intensity I could manage along with my favorite tapes on the car stereo, and staring out at the church cemetery. I thought about how in the Bible Jesus had once said "Lazarus, come forth," and Lazarus had risen from the dead and come forth. If Jesus had just said "Come forth," everyone in the graveyard would have come forth.

I tried an experiment to see if I was the Second Coming. *Come forth,* I thought toward the graves.

A little voice in my head said *not yet.* I was immensely relieved that nothing more than that happened. If someone had knocked on the car window at that moment, I would have freaked out.

People had shown a real tendency to do the opposite of what I wanted. During this time the ultranationalist Russian politician Vladimir Zhirinovsky was making headlines with his dangerous ideas, and I couldn't help but oppose him. The more I opposed him, though, it seemed the more popular he became with his countrymen. I wondered if he might rise to power simply because I opposed him, and lead the world to its own destruction because of me.

It's just 'Novsky, thought people. *He's not so bad. In fact, I even think I kind of like him, since you don't.*

November found me cursing my fate at having to make such a

horrible decision. If I was telepathic, then opening fire on my tormentors would be the best thing I could do. It would be self-defense, and might even help save the world from the madness of others. If I turned out not to be telepathic, though, I would probably be killed, or at least wounded and sent to a prison or a mental hospital for a very long time, and innocent people would have died. I would be hated and reviled, and any subsequent explanation of what my motives had been would be nearly unfathomable to the uninitiated. No, in that event by far the best thing to do would be to go back on my medication. A comparison of worst-case scenarios had made me realize that I just couldn't take that chance, though. What if the entire human race was really in danger? It seemed that offering myself and a few other people as insurance against the destruction of the world was the only moral thing I could do, even if the chance that the world would really be destroyed was relatively small. It was the magnitude of the potential calamity, not its probability, that made that risk intolerable.

I had learned in my childhood religious instruction that near the end of the world, there would be a coming-together of nations, and peace would reign for a time. The collapse of the Soviet Union and the new peace between Jews and Arabs made it appear that this was coming to pass, and all at a time when mankind nonetheless had the power to destroy himself. What if it was God's plan that the first telepath should also be the last, a harbinger of the end of time for all mankind? What if He meant for me to be the Second Coming of Christ? I cursed Him for putting me in the position of having to decide whether such a thing was true, and if it was, then I was rebelling against Him. I would not forgive my tormentors as Jesus had. I would not take the commandment "thou shalt not kill" and live by it. I would not let them say that I was Jesus. I would prove them wrong, so that the world would live on. In any event, whether I was telepathic or not, the world would live on. That was my decision.

I worried that it would live on while I spent the rest of my own life behind prison walls. That to me would be a fate worse than death. I could die at the hands of the police and not complain, for by that time I would have killed, too. I could die by lethal injection some time later and still not complain, for the same reason. But life imprisonment—that would be too much!

If I were you and I got life in prison for doing what you're about to do, I would just lie about and relax and repose and rest, thought Bill Clinton.

This comforted me. Yes, if I got life in prison I would just lie about and relax and repose.

And rest, thought Bill Clinton.

And rest, I agreed. Yes, that would be all right. I liked to rest, and I supposed I could rest peacefully knowing that I had done my best to do the right thing. My mission in life would have been fulfilled.

But still I cursed God for making that my mission in life.

The internet was first becoming popular in those days, and people silently called my telepathy another *internet.* They were using my service and paying no fees. They had the perfect little setup, I thought. Just run roughshod over Wendell and if he tries to assert himself, just say he's mentally ill and that he needs help.

Often when I communicated with General Schwarzkopf, I would get the smell of model glue and paint thinner. I thought he was doing it because he thought all I knew about the military was what I had learned from building model tanks and warplanes when I was younger. It was kind of funny, really, his showing his contempt for me in that way. He warned me, *don't get bajuggered,* meaning captured alive. I thought it was good advice. I would force the police to kill me on the spot if they dared, and if they didn't, well then we would all know something. That was the reason I wanted so much ammunition, so I could hold out for days, if necessary, if the police didn't dare to kill me. That would give people a little time to rethink their position on me, which they would have to do because you just can't have a man with a high-powered rifle and lots and lots of ammunition running around killing people at will, with no one daring to stop him. I would have to stay awake all that time, though, or risk getting "bajuggered." That would be bad.

The police had guns. If I went around claiming out loud to be telepathic, all people had to do was call the police and I would have to do as the police said. That had happened more times than I could remember, since all this craziness had started. I won't even bother you with a list of my police run-ins. If they and everyone else were really as dangerous as I suspected, why shouldn't I arm myself as well? After all, if I was really telepathic, then these people were damaging my left shoulder as surely as with a bullet. My physical pain left me no choice. I had to arm myself and act while the shoulder was still mobile. I would be fighting to protect my shoulder, and to protect the world from the people who would tear my shoulder up just because they could, and get away with it. After all, the notion that this experience with my shoulder was caused by mental illness seemed at least as farfetched as the notion that I was extremely telepathic, from which much followed. Decidedly important if true.

And if I was going to arm myself, why not go all the way and arm myself with a truly fearsome weapon, my father's M-1?

It's a Saturday Night Special, sang the alien thoughts mockingly to the tune of a Lynyrd Skynyrd song. *Got a barrel that's blue and cold.*

In mid-November I went to a gun show in Raleigh, intending to buy whatever I thought would be useful, and to show people (without actually telling them, of course) that I was serious. There I found a good deal on 8-round clips for the M-1 rifle, and I bought about 50 of them.

Good luck, the man who sold them to me thought. *I hope you never have to use them.*

Me too, I silently replied. *By the way, this would be an excellent time for you to come clean about this little thing we all have for hearing each other's thoughts.*

He seemed pained. *Okay, you're telepathic,* he thought.

No, no, don't say it up here, say it out there, I thought.

But that would make it all true.

It's already true, you fool.

Good attitude. I need that vibrator. Goddammit, I'm trying but I just can't help but think of that thing you used to use. Do what you gotta do, is all I can say.

I thanked him pleasantly and left. I also bought an Army backpack and some canvas bags with straps. They would be for carrying my ammunition.

I also went to a gun store in Hillsborough. There I found what looked like an M-14, an impressive weapon used by the U.S. military in Korea and Vietnam. I asked the proprietor about it, and he said it was an M-1A, which differed from the M-14 only in that it was a semiautomatic and not capable of fully automatic fire. I thought it would make an excellent purchase, and decided to return in January as soon as I got my money.

Then I went to Fayetteville, N.C. I thought there would probably be some good gun stores near Fort Bragg, and I found one right on Bragg Boulevard. They had a number of 20-round magazines for the M-1A, and I bought them all. I still had a little money left, so I thought about driving that same day to Jacksonville, N.C. to see if there were any good gun stores near the Marine base at Camp Lejeune. I pulled out my road map and realized how far away it was, reachable from Fayetteville only by secondary roads. *That's too far,* I thought.

From here to eternity, thought General Schwarzkopf, who had been listening to me think about those two big military bases all day.

For Thanksgiving I returned to my parents' house. There my mother was worried about me, and asked about my medication. I told her I might have to go back on it. I told her that just to get her to leave me alone. *You know what I'm really planning to do,* I thought toward her. *What do you think about that?*

Fahrvergnugen, came her only response. At the time I thought it meant "well-engineered" or something like that, but someone has since told me it means "the driving experience." Oh well.

Back in Chapel Hill, people were still thinking *you're not really going to do this thing. I just thought I'd tell you.*

Oh yes I am, I thought toward one man. I tried hard to convince him of the folly of denying any longer that I was telepathic, but he clung to his former prejudices anyway.

Look, he thought, *I've already decided how I'm going to be about this thing, so it's up to you to prove me wrong.*

I tried to find out why they were so obstinate, but all they would tell me was *I don't want to do without my love. What will I do if I lose my love? You're not really going to do this thing.*

Sometimes people would think *he'd kill every one of us if he knew.*

I even went so far as to try to sabotage ahead of time any possible use of the insanity defense, by claiming out loud to strangers that I could kill someone and be found not guilty by reason of insanity, just so long as I established my insanity ahead of time. I did this so that after I killed, they would have to give me the death penalty or admit that I was a special case.

People sometimes silently called me a *Marine*. This was designed just to irritate me, because I had wanted to join the Army, not the Marines. It was like calling my rifle a *shotgun*, or a hamburger a *sandwich*, or any of the other things they said. One night Clint McRory thought *you may not be a Marine, but I'd give you my Silver Star just for what you've already been through.* About this time I was wondering when to stop killing people once I started, and had decided I wouldn't be able to stop until people had admitted beyond retraction that I was telepathic, that they had wronged me, that they were afraid to kill me, and that they wouldn't prosecute me for murder. Only then would I safely be able to stop killing them. That was why I needed so much ammunition.

If I get that far, I'll deserve the Congressional Medal of Honor, I thought to Clint.

He just laughed. *Maybe so*, he thought. *In any event, you're going to like the new you.* He kept thinking that whenever I thought about what I was going to do. *You're going to like the new you.*

"He's an American," someone said out loud.

If I was right, and if my grim task was successful, the rewards would be tremendous. Perhaps Congress would make an exception to the rules and in fact award me a Medal of Honor to placate me for the horrible, ungodly risk I had had to take. Perhaps someday there would even be a Nobel Peace Prize as my ideas for world unity caught on with the entire human race the easy way, without the bother of everyone having to read everything I had read and learn everything I had learned to support those ideas, without any language barriers or time lost. They would just know, because I was telepathic. Perhaps even the ideas themselves would improve, as others chose to make the most of my telepathic potential, educate me in the areas of my interest, and correct any misconceptions I had. At the time all of this seemed like a realistically possible outcome.

I wanted that Medal of Honor. I found it aesthetically appealing, shaped as it was like a Satanic pentagram and featuring the head of Minerva, the Roman goddess of war. A real bitch, I was sure. Also, the medal would give more meaning to my actions. I would approach the world as a deeply affronted conquering warrior, not as some passive, long-suffering religious figure, as people seemed to want to picture me. *I'll make you people think Minerva*, I thought.

Minerve endings, they thought back.

I suppose there will be military people who read this and think I'm scum who doesn't even deserve to look at a Medal of Honor, let alone own one. Believe me, I know what this decoration means. That is why I latched on to it as being the one reward that could make worthwhile all this suffering and moral and physical courage I felt I was being forced to display.

Of course if I was wrong, then my grim task would be rewarded only with a prison cell or a mental hospital ward, with only the knowledge that I had done my best as consolation. For that reason, I had to be absolutely certain that performing the task really was the best I could do to do the right thing. And for that reason, I thought, if I went through with this I deserved the damn medal just for effort and intention. Am I making sense?

On "In Utero" there is a song called "tourettes," which begins with the spoken words "moderate rock." Kurt Cobain then screams what sounded to me like the following lyrics:

Bitch try to ruin me
No way
Cut it out around the town
My arm
Wendell don't, it's a test
My own
Wendell don't, say that fast
My arm, hey

Out of time on the phone
It's my own
Wendell don't, it's a test
My arm
Whoa no, hit the phone
My arm, hey

Mean heart, cold heart
Cold heart, cold heart
Cold heart, cold heart
Cold heart, cold eye, eh?

That was exactly the kind of talk I had been trying to capture with my camcorder, and here it was even set to music for me.

In December I took exams for the last time. I hadn't studied at all during the semester, but I had attended nearly every class. I just wrote my opinions to how the law was for each question, and cited no authority. I thought it would probably be good enough to pass, but not much more.

As soon as I finished writing my last exam, I packed up my car and drove to Connecticut, where an old college friend named Kirk had invited me for the holidays. I intended to say nothing about what was going on with me, in the hopes he or his family would bring it up first and thereby admit that they knew what I was thinking. On my second day there Kirk did mention that he'd heard from another mutual friend that I was having some mental problems. I said I didn't want to talk about it, and he didn't say anything else. I didn't really blame him. I assumed he knew what was going on, but like everyone else was waiting for someone else to say it.

Kirk and I went to his brother Brion's house in New York state. There I met Brion's wife, and the four of us partied for days. We went to Woodstock, which is kind of a Mecca to the kind of music that I loved but blamed for getting me into this whole mess of being telepathic. There were shops with T-shirts and posters showing every rock star whose songs I had ever learned, it seemed, including my old buddies, John Lennon and Jimi Hendrix. Everybody was still talking about the big festival in 1969, and it seemed the whole town was still caught in that time frame. I liked it, and thought Annetta would have, too, if she had been there.

I spent Christmas at Kirk's parents' home in Connecticut. They were fun people, and I really enjoyed the change from my usual Christmas routine with my own family. As always, I did my best not to let on like anything was wrong, hoping they would say something about my telepathy anyway, but they didn't.

After Christmas Kirk and I went with Brion to a cabin Brion was building in the Adirondacks. There was about a foot of snow on the ground, and we spent several days cutting pine trees and burning them on huge bonfires, trying to clear the land so the cabin could be seen. It was fun work, and I was surprised to find that my shoulder wasn't giving me the trouble it had been.

That's because you know what you're going to do about it, Brion thought.

If it stays this healthy, I might not have to do anything at all about it, I thought hopefully.

Yeah, well, if you decide not to do anything, can't you picture that shoulder just going to shit? Brion thought. *Can't you picture people making it just collapse?*

I agreed. No, there was no getting around this ghastly test which lay just ahead of me, now only a month off. I hoped with all my heart that it would go well for me, that the police would be afraid to shoot me and that people would have to admit at last that they had been dreadfully wrong in their approach to my gift.

For New Year's Kirk and I went to New York to be in Times Square for the dropping of the ball. Everyone in New York seemed to know all about me. *We're waiting for you,* they would think.

Why don't you spare me the trouble of killing people and just admit now what's going on? I thought.

Because of what we've already done, they replied.

Don't you see how you all deserve to die for this? I wondered.

Hey, I just did what I was told, they would think. *That thing came along and took me by the hand and showed me how to get myself some, so I did. No big deal. And she was fantastic, man. That's really some gift you have, to know what she's thinking while you're putting it to her. I saw what this was all about.*

I just shook my head and went on. Aside from what I heard them thinking, though, the people in New York seemed very friendly and cheerful, I suppose because it was New Year's Eve. I thought they were doing a masterful job of feigning their ignorance, but then, I was doing a masterful job of doing the same thing.

Kirk and I celebrated until the early morning hours of 1995, wandering the streets of Manhattan and Greenwich Village with bottles of champagne. I was thrilled that my big year had finally arrived, and Kirk was just thrilled.

A few hours later we took the train back to Connecticut where my car was waiting. On the way I saw a man and a boy standing together, and the boy thought *please do something. He's hurting me.* There was nothing I could do right then, but I swore I would remember this moment when the time came. And I did.

At midafternoon of New Year's Day, 1995 I started the long drive back to the North Carolina mountains, and arrived on January 2. My student loan money wouldn't be available until the 11th, so I had more than a week to just wait around nervously.

I worked on writing songs, and watched the civil war in Chechnya on the news at night. I learned that the Russians had been following tactics I had silently recommended to General Schwarzkopf, of keeping infantry in their armored vehicles while they moved forward to keep the soldiers from being hit by small-arms fire. This turned out not to be a good idea, because many of them were killed by rocket-propelled grenades while still in their vehicles. The U.S. Army way of doing things would have been to dismount the infantry to neutralize the enemy grenadiers, and assume some small-arms fire casualties. I felt like the Russian debacle was my fault, that I shouldn't have recommended using their infantry that way, and that the whole thing was further destabilizing Russia to Zhirinovsky's advantage. I silently promised the dejected-looking Russian prisoners I saw not to worry, that the world would be a very different place in a few weeks anyway. A lot of them looked younger than I was, and I was concerned about them.

Just to prove to people that I was still serious about my plans to make them regret what they had done to me, I bought several boxes of ammunition for the M-1A. The man I bought them from thought *I just thought I'd tell you, you're wasting your money.*

What do you mean? I wondered.

I mean, you're not really going to do this thing, he thought.

Motherfucker, I'll come in here and blow your head off and take all your ammunition.

I need that vibrator. You'll be too scared. I know you.

You're as wrong as you could be, I thought. *I mean to do this thing.*

Good attitude was his only reply.

One night I was sitting in front of the small television in my parents' kitchen, wondering what the police were really going to do when I came at them firing my rifle. A friend I hadn't heard from in a long time thought *I'll tell you what they'll do. They'll freak out and jizz on their vibrators, is what they'll do.*

I returned to Chapel Hill, picked up my student loan check, cashed it, and bought the M-1A. At every transaction everyone silently assured me that they weren't scared, that they knew I wouldn't go through with it. They thought I was just bluffing, and they weren't buying it. They silently told me they had too much at stake to ever admit I was telepathic. I silently told them they would die if they didn't. They refused to budge, and it was the same as I took my enormous amount of money around to every gun store I could find and bought them all out of ammunition for the M-1A and the M-1. I was ready to tell them I was a hunter, but they didn't ask. They seemed to know what it was for, anyway. In fact, a man at a gun store in Hillsborough said, "Now I don't want to see you up in the Bell Tower shooting at people with that thing."

"Oh, don't worry about that," I said, laughing. *I'll be down on the street with it,* I thought. Why would he warn me not to do something like that if he didn't already know what I was planning? Also, I soon noticed after I got this rifle that people weren't giving me the trouble telepathically that they had before, which made me think I was on the right track in resorting to violence. For the first time, they seemed to be taking me and my plan seriously.

In mid-January I took all my weaponry to my mother's uninhabited farm in the mountains of east Tennessee. It was the ideal training ground, 350 acres of mostly wooded mountainside where I could sleep in the old farmhouse and not be bothered by anyone. It was cold, several inches of snow on the ground, and I didn't expect any visitors in that kind of weather.

One of the first discoveries I made in my "training" was that some of the 20-round magazines I had bought for the M-1A were defective. I would fire one round and the magazine would partially eject, forcing me to reposition it and fire each round individually. I was glad I hadn't discovered this when the real deal hit the fan. I took those magazines back to the gunstore where I had bought them and ordered the more expensive, name-brand Springfield magazines, which worked as they should.

Every time I fired a round, I pretended I was actually shooting a person, to get myself used to the idea. It really cut against the grain of everything I had ever been taught about gun safety, but I just pretended I was a combat soldier in training and that there was a war on. I had to reach down and find within myself whatever steeliness I would otherwise have used only if I were a combat soldier.

In all of this my old friend Clint McRory became a valuable advisor. Time and time again he encouraged me to do things I hadn't thought of, such as practicing carrying different amounts of ammunition on my back to the top of the Bull Mountain and back, both to get myself in shape and also to teach me what the optimal amount of ammunition would be when the time came. On the first night I did this, wearing all my brand-new equipment and with soft warm insoles in my boots, I stepped in an icy mud puddle and soaked my foot. It was a very unpleasant sensation, and Hillary Clinton thought *aw, he's from Atlanta.* She meant that my upbringing was too suburban for this kind of activity, and it was funny. I kept going, pretending to shoot at imaginary enemies all around me so I could get used to twisting my torso with all that weight on my back. After a while of climbing the mountain, twisting around, and pretending to fire my rifle, an alien male thought said *that's a total body workout, isn't it?* It was. I was soon panting and sweating like a horse despite the cold.

I had trouble with the laces to my boots coming untied while I was rushing around like that, and it was hard to retie them with all that gear on my back. *We used to use something for that problem when I was in the Marines,* Clint McRory thought one night as I was struggling for the umpteenth time to tie my boots without letting go of the rifle in my hands. *It's called "duct tape."* I started wrapping duct tape around the laces, and they stayed tied.

During these training sessions the female thoughts would say *you can consider this part completely de-segued.* They called my ammunition bags *segue bags,* and called loading my rifle *segueing the ammunition.* I got used to this nomenclature, and began using it myself sometimes. After much practice I realized that it was a little bit faster and easier to segue the ammunition to the M-1 than to the M-1A, because the M-1 automatically ejected clips when they were empty, whereas the M-1A required that you pull those long 20-round magazines out, put the empty magazine away, and then reload. Besides, the M-1 clips were inexpensive and therefore expendable, whereas the 20-round magazines cost forty bucks apiece and had to be saved. For these reasons I decided to use the M-1 when the time came, because I figured the added speed in reloading would allow me to keep up a faster overall rate of fire, even though I would have to reload more often. The female thoughts in my head called the 8-round clips *birds,* because of the way they felt smaller and more delicate, especially when I was wearing the heavy cowhide gloves I had bought in New York state a few weeks earlier to wear while clearing Brion's land. I had found them also helpful now, not only because of the cold, but also because constantly reloading high-powered rifles in a hurry can skin your hands up.

The nights up at that farm were scary. It was freezing and the wind would blow, causing doors in the old barns to slam again and again. Somewhere a piece of a tin roof needed to be nailed down, and it would rattle in the breeze. I thought about how, if I did this thing and was wrong about being telepathic, I would probably be killed. I might have only a few days left to live, even now, and I didn't want to die! I wanted to accomplish a great positive out of my situation and live happily ever after.

One night I lay awake in the rusty old bed and wondered if I was really the Second Coming of Christ, and if it was all part of God's will that the world should end. How could I fight against that? What if events had already become unstoppable, or would have led to the end no matter what I had done from the very beginning? Outside the wind blew harder and I shivered. I thought about the old pioneer cemetery down the lane, and silently commanded to the corpses, *come forth.*

There was silence, and then a voice in my head said *they'll come forth when the time comes.*

All I knew for certain was that something terrible was happening to my mind, and that in a few days people would die by my hand. Perhaps I would be killed or wounded or captured and sent to a prison or a mental hospital, and forever lose control of my fate. It would have been so much easier at that point just to return to Chapel Hill and start my classes like I had been doing for so long, but I just didn't think that was the right thing to do anymore. I had to know if I was telepathic and if I really had this horrifying relationship with the rest of humanity. I tried to close negative thoughts out of my mind and have courage, but it was so very, very hard.

Whatever it was that was happening to me, it was an absolute outrage. That much I knew. If it was mental illness, it was also a damned convincing impression of mental telepathy, and it had put me in the position of being rationally and morally forced to bet everything that I was on the hope that I could completely trust my senses.

I usually did my main training after dark so no one would accidentally discover me running around playing army. One dark and windy night as I was getting ready to begin training again, I discovered that one of the shoulder straps on my backpack had come undone. It was at a complicated fastening, and it was hard to see how it had come undone without anybody doing it intentionally. As I was fumbling with the strap there in the dark, an alien thought said *Wendell, I don't know if you believe in witchcraft, but I'm beginning to, and I think you should leave off this whole vibrator adventure right now, before it goes any farther.* I was scared, because I didn't really know what was happening to me, and I didn't see how the strap could have come undone like that by itself, but I promised myself that I wouldn't give up my plan. It seemed like people were just trying to discourage me with their thoughts because they were beginning to see how serious I was. That, I felt, was progress, and maybe they would yet admit that I was telepathic without anyone's blood having to be spilled. I got the strap fixed, duct-taped it to keep that from happening again, and went on with my practice exercise.

In the last week of January I returned to Chapel Hill for the final time. I planned to cache out most of my ammunition in isolated locations, so I could pick it up 200 rounds at a time as needed. As I was caching it out, the female voices said I was *seguing out my ammo.* I segued most of my ammo near Jordan Lake, with about 200 rounds in the UNC Botanical Gardens and another 200 rounds in the woods near my old apartment. I would carry 600 rounds with me, which was really too much, but I was afraid I would have to do a lot of shooting before I got to another ammo segue. In all I had about a thousand rounds for each rifle. I segued the M-1A at Jordan lake with eleven loaded 20-round magazines, but I kept the trigger assembly in my backpack in case someone found the rest of the rifle. By January 25 I had spent nearly all of my money on weapons, equipment, and ammunition. On that day I spent another fifteen dollars on a military gas mask from Surplus Sid's, in case the police had thoughts of lobbing tear gas grenades at me so they wouldn't have to shoot me.

That night I went out one last time to have a few beers at Linda's. It would be these people's next to last chance to admit that I was telepathic. As usual, the evidence was all around me, but nobody was admitting anything. They all seemed to think I would chicken out, and besides, none of them planned to be on Henderson Street the next day anyway. Just before I left I ran into Logan, the old drummer in my friend Dmitri's band. We chatted a while. I told him it was my last semester of law school, and that I was thinking about going to Asheville after I graduated to teach English at my old boarding school. He seemed to think it was a good idea, and while he was saying so he was thinking *yeah, that's what you better do, because if you start shooting at people tomorrow, those cops are going to blow you away. We'll never admit you can read people's minds.* I finished my beer and left.

I then walked through the route I would take. There had been a home basketball game between Carolina and Florida State that night, and for a time I had considered opening fire on the crowd as they left the game. I decided not to do that for several reasons. First, there would be children present, and children were fine with me. Second, it would mean having to shoot a large number of people before there would be any indication of whether the police would kill me or not, being dark and all, and that wouldn't serve to prove my point very well soon enough. A bloodbath like that wouldn't be necessary to the goal I hoped to accomplish. I decided instead to park my car below Henderson Street the next day, in broad daylight, and walk up that street looking for people to shoot. I knew Henderson Street at midday would have a moderate number of people out and about, and I figured I would be able to kill enough of them before reaching Franklin Street and its hordes of cops and students to force the police to shoot to kill once I got there, if they dared. If they didn't dare, I would cut a deadly swath across campus until I reached the Botanical Gardens and my next ammo segue, then go over to the defensive and try to stay awake until the newspapers told the whole truth about why I was able to do all of this and still stay alive and unhurt. That, I thought, might take days and dozens of killings. It was what people seemed to want, though, so it was what they were going to get.

The next morning I slept late, then got up, showered, and drove to McDonald's on Franklin Street to park my car. All of my assault paraphernalia was in the trunk, all legally packaged away in case the police stopped me at the last moment. I was ready with a story about planning to go to the mountains that weekend to target shoot and leave all that stuff there. If the police stopped me now, I would know for sure that something was up, and they knew I knew that, so they didn't stop me. At least that's how I interpreted the situation. As always, I couldn't really be sure.

I ate lunch at Bruegger's Bagels, and had a cup of coffee. The place was a lot more crowded than usual, and I thought everyone wanted to be there to see if someone else would publicly admit that they could hear my thoughts. No one had the guts to do this, and with all that ammunition in my car, I didn't want to say anything that would give someone the excuse to have me committed again. That would blow the whole thing.

I did plenty of thinking at other people, though, reminding them that this was positively their last chance to stop this madness before somebody really got hurt. *You're really going to shoot those people, aren't you?* one girl thought.

Yes I am, I silently answered.

Ooh, how creepy, she silently replied. I finished my coffee and left.

From that point on, I heard no one's thoughts but my own. This made me think people were just trying to fool me like they had with the Navane, trying to convince me at the eleventh hour that I wasn't really telepathic so that I wouldn't shoot them. My mind was just as quiet as it had been when I was on my medication. This made me madder than ever. I was scared, but I was also mad, and it also all made me even more sure I was on the right track.

Once I was out of Bruegger's, I knew any further hesitation would just make me more nervous than I needed to be, so I walked resolutely back to my car in the McDonald's parking lot. When I got to it I got in, wrapped duct tape around my boot laces, and pulled out. I drove to my prearranged spot at the bottom of Henderson Street, half expecting to be pulled over and searched at any moment. No one pulled me over, so again I thought they didn't want to tip me off.

I parked at the foot of the steps leading to Henderson Street and got out. A middle-aged black man started walking toward me. I got out of the car, opened the trunk, and quickly put on my segue bags and backpack. The last thing I pulled out was the M-1 rifle from its carrying case. Once it was out in the sunlight I knew I was at the point of no return. From here on, every move I made would put me deeper into trouble if I was wrong about being telepathic.

I loaded the rifle, and the middle-aged black man stopped abruptly. I could have killed him there where he stood, but I didn't because he was black and I had no particular animosity toward black people. They had always seemed nice enough, ever since the telepathy had started, but they just hadn't taken the all-important step of publicly admitting I was a telepath. I walked right past him and climbed the steps.

My heart was pounding. I knew I would kill the next person I saw. Up the street I saw some people, and I walked toward them. The walk seemed to take forever. I saw a man at his mailbox turn and head toward the front of his house. I raised the rifle, aimed it at his chest, and squeezed the trigger, expecting a rifle that powerful to kill him instantly.

The rifle roared, but the man just staggered slightly and then hurried up the steps toward his front door. I shot him a second time in the chest, and he fell down. Then he moaned a terrible, heart-wrenching moan of despair. I shot him a third time and he stopped moaning. I had just killed a man.

A young woman saw all of this, and quickly hid behind a car. I took pity on her, and told her to run away so I wouldn't shoot her. She did as I suggested.

Up the street some students were riding their bicycles toward me. I shot at the biggest one, a tall, athletic-looking young man. He fell off of his bicycle and started trying to crawl under a car. I shot him a second time and he moaned just like the first man had, a terrible moan of despair. I shot him a third time, and like the first man he stopped moaning then. I had just killed two men.

Somewhere in the distance I heard a police siren. I had already fired six of my eight rounds in the first clip, so I hurried into a little cul-de-sac to reload. I pressed the clip eject button, and the two last rounds popped out with the empty clip, ringing as they hit the ground. I slammed another clip into the rifle, and stepped back out into the street just as the police car was going past. I fired all eight rounds through the back windshield, as fast as I could pull the trigger. The police car swerved across the Rosemary Street intersection, collided with a parked car on the other side of the street, and came to a stop with its blue lights still flashing.

I rapidly reloaded. Next to the Henderson Street Bar was a beer truck, and I tried to kill the driver as he scrambled out of the truck and into the bar. Up on the hill to my right a group of students pointed at me and yelled, "There he is. Get him! Get him!" I emptied my rifle at them and they ran away.

I continued up the street, reloading and firing as I went. Someone, or maybe it was two people, tried to get at the police officer trapped in the shot-up cruiser. I fired over the cruiser at them, under it, and through it, but I didn't think I was hitting anyone. Some more police officers appeared behind a concrete wall behind the post office building and opened fire at me. I heard bullets flying to my left and thought they were just trying to intimidate me, that surely they wouldn't dare to shoot the world's only telepath. I fired back at them, and we exchanged shots for what seemed like an eternity, but which probably only lasted a few seconds. I started forward to drive them away, and a bullet hit the toe of my right boot. I fired again, and a bullet hit the calf of my right leg.

It didn't hurt much, but I screamed anyway because I was suddenly very much alarmed. So they dared to shoot me after all! That leg was going to need medical attention, but I continued to return fire. I got off maybe two or three shots, and then another bullet hit me just above the left ankle, shattering the bone. I tried to take another step, but the broken leg wouldn't hold my weight, and I fell in a heap there in the middle of Henderson Street, segue bags and all.

I hesitated. I could now fight it out to the death or go to prison, possibly for the rest of my life. There was no doubt in my mind that if I tried to reload again I would immediately be splattered all over the asphalt by a hail of bullets.

Maybe prison won't be that bad, I thought. I yelled, "All right! I give up!"

A heavy silence fell. Behind me I heard footsteps, and I turned to see someone running out of the Henderson Street Bar toward me. My savior, I thought. He grabbed my rifle and tossed it aside, then got on top of me to hold me down. I didn't struggle.

Police emerged seemingly from all directions and converged on me at once. They slapped on handcuffs, then debated for a moment over what to do about all the equipment that was strapped to me. Someone produced an enormous knife, and a police officer cut off my segue bags and backpack. They tried to stand me up and I screamed again, this time because of the pain of my broken leg. Someone pushed through the crowd and punched me in the face, knocking off my glasses. The police rushed me into a waiting police cruiser and slammed the door. All around me students and other people had gathered to gawk, and I felt embarrassed. I had blood all over me, and had to hold my left leg just a certain way to keep the pain from my broken bones from becoming completely unbearable.

"Where are we going?" asked the driver.

"To the police station," said the officer beside me.

"I think I've been shot," I said.

"Take us to the hospital," said the officer beside me.

"I forgot my radio," said the driver. "Let's go to the station first so I can pick it up."

I listened to the car's police scanner as we rode toward the station. Through the static I heard people saying things like, "He did it. That thing did it." I listened more closely, and they said, "No, don't hold me." My heart rose. Maybe I was telepathic after all. Maybe I could still get them to admit it.

At the police station the driver went inside to get her radio, and the officer beside me started gasping for breath. "I'll be all right," he said. "I just realized what just happened."

When he recovered he read me my rights, and we sped off toward UNC Memorial Hospital a mile away.

At the emergency room there was chaos. They lifted me out of the police cruiser and into a wheelchair, and I screamed as they shifted my shattered leg. They brought me inside, and a young man with a bullet through his shoulder said, "Gotcha."

I couldn't think of any witty comeback, so I just said, "Yes, sir." They put me on a bed, and cut off my jeans. They tried to remove the boots but were having trouble with that because of the duct tape around the laces. They asked me why I had duct tape around my laces, and I told them so they wouldn't come untied. They finally got the duct tape off and removed the bloody boots. I asked them to prop up my left foot so it wouldn't flop over, which they did.

Everyone was talking about what had just happened. "They're still finding people where they've been shot and crawled away," someone said. "There's no telling how many there are going to be."

A nurse told me one of the men I had shot had died. She said it like she was really breaking some bad news to me, but I was not surprised at all. In fact, once I had a moment to myself, my first instinct was to breathe a sigh of relief that it was over, that I had done it, that everyone had been wrong about me, and that someone had died as a result. I felt Medal-of-Honor proud.

After a while they wheeled me into the X-ray room and took X-rays of my legs. I was very alarmed when I saw the X-ray of my lower left leg. Both bones were shattered into many pieces, seemingly beyond repair. I was afraid they would have to amputate my foot, but still I felt proud of my actions, even though it hadn't turned out as I had hoped.

I don't remember being taken to a private room, but after a time I ended up in one. Someone asked me if I wanted to call my family and tell them what had happened, but I refused. My family were the last people in the world I wanted to talk to right then. I blamed them for not having the good sense to admit that I was telepathic before this horrible thing happened. Or, if I wasn't telepathic, then I was too ashamed of myself for having been so wrong. I didn't know which way I should be, but in my heart of hearts I knew I had done the best I could. That was why I felt privately proud.

I had a police officer in my room there in the hospital 24 hours a day. Together we watched the news, and from what I gathered from watching the reports of the shooting in Chapel Hill, this deed had caught people completely by surprise. No reporter gave away the slightest hint that everyone had known for months that this was going to happen. My hopes began to sink again. There was no telephone call from Bill Clinton saying he had known this was going to happen, that I was a telepath and a hero.

That night I had surgery on my left leg. Beforehand, the surgeon explained that he would put a metal rod into the leg to hold the bones in place, and that if I didn't have the surgery, there was about a 70% chance that amputation would be necessary. I consented to the operation.

Before they put me under anesthesia, I think they were expecting a struggle, but I put up no resistance.

Over the next few days I had lots of visitors. There was a psychiatrist who listened to my story and asked questions. "What do we mean when we say a rolling stone gathers no moss? That people in glass houses shouldn't throw stones? Who's the President of the United States? How far is it from New York to Paris?" After I had answered to the best of my ability, he prescribed the antipsychotic drug Haldol. I saw no harm in taking it at this late date. There were lawyers, Kirk Osborn and James Williams, who said they would pursue an insanity defense. There was a psychologist named Dr. Warren who listened to my whole story, asking questions, and seeming very concerned about me. There was an investigator from the State Bureau of Investigation, who seemed most concerned about why I had chosen Henderson Street as the place to begin my attack. I told him that it really had made no difference where I started, and that I could have shot up the UNC basketball game against Florida State on January 25 if I had so chosen. I told him everybody was equally to blame for the shooting, and so it made no difference who actually ended up paying for it with their lives.

I also had a visit from my mother, who cried, and my sister SusAnnetta, who didn't. SusAnnetta was an attorney in Tennessee. I told them why I had done it, and asked a lot of questions of SusAnnetta about life in prison, because the police officer in my room had told me that would be my next stop, and SusAnnetta knew a lot about prisons from her criminal defense work. She told me it was not really a confrontational environment, but that I should nevertheless be careful who I associated with, that I should not go up and talk to people I didn't know, and I should under no circumstances buy drugs on credit. She said that people eventually got used to being in prison, and went about their daily lives there just like people on the outside.

I asked her about the death penalty, which I was hoping to get if I got convicted. She said not to place my hopes in that, and that even if I got sentenced to death, I might spend ten or fifteen years sitting on death row while all the mandatory appeals went forward. That news was discouraging. I also asked if she thought there would be tapes of what the police had said on the radio during and immediately after the attack, because I thought these might help me prove I was telepathic and that what I had done had been justified.

On my third day in the hospital, a physical therapist came to my room and began teaching me how to use crutches. We went up and down the hall a few times, which caused me tremendous pain. I didn't see how in the world I would be ready to make the trip to Central Prison on the scheduled date of January 30. We kept working on it, though, and on January 30 I went to Central Prison to await trial.

That morning they woke me up early, gave me some ugly and ill-fitting polyester clothes someone had found lying around the hospital somewhere, and told me it was time to go. They wheeled me in a wheelchair down the hall and into an elevator, then down another hall and out to a waiting police car. We rode first back to the Chapel Hill police station where I was to be photographed and fingerprinted. I felt miserable, both because of the pain of my wounds, and because I am not a morning person anyway. I just wanted to lie down somewhere and go back to sleep.

The fingerprinting process took forever because there had to be fingerprints for every charge against me, and everyone was expecting lots of charges. Afterward they gave me some harsh abrasive soap to wash the ink off my hands, but it was only marginally effective. I crutched my painful way in leg irons back out to the police car, feeling like death warmed over, and there stood a television reporter with a cameraman.

"Mr. Williamson, why did you do it?" she called out.

I was stuck for an answer. How could I tell the whole story in one five-second sound bite? "My attorneys told me not to comment on the case," I said. My attorneys later had a fit over my even saying that much.

We got into the police car and left for Raleigh.

At the entrance to Central Prison there was another reporter and another cameraman. They didn't ask any questions, but just kept filming me as I sat there in the car. I thought about smiling and waving, because I was feeling better by that time in the morning, but I didn't do it because I didn't want to incur the wrath of my attorneys. The gate opened and we drove inside.

There were several gates, and at one the sheriff's deputies who were driving me there had to leave their handguns. No handguns were allowed in Central Prison, even on the persons of law enforcement authorities. We drove through the last gate and stopped in front of a big metal door.

The sheriff's deputies told me to come with them, and I crutched my way inside. They motioned me into a little room with cold metal benches all around the walls, and took off my handcuffs and leg irons. After a while a prison guard came by and told me to strip. He searched me and my meager belongings, telling me to squat and cough, etc. Then they gave me a thin blue hospital gown and paper sandals, and told me to wait while they processed me in.

After a while they told me to come on, and they led me to an elevator. Upstairs they put me in a tiny metal holding cage and gave me lunch. It was two hot dogs, baked beans, and a half pint of milk from the N.C. State dairy. It was surprisingly good.

When I finished eating, they led me out of the holding cage and down a series of long corridors. I was having trouble keeping up on my crutches, and the guards had to stop and wait for me from time to time. Finally we got to the Central Prison hospital, where they put me in a room with four other inmates. I lay down on my bed and pretty soon I was asleep.

It is well known that the press tends to sensationalize, and my case was no exception. In the days following the shooting every aspect of my personality was distorted by the news media, aided by people who knew me only peripherally and who themselves probably had distorted perceptions of what I was like. People who knew me well didn't talk at all to the media for fear of saying something that might be held against me by the justice system.

The press even distorted the objectively verifiable facts. For example, it was widely reported that I had been wearing sunglasses and camouflage fatigues at the time of the shooting, when in reality I had worn blue jeans, a black tee shirt, a gray coat, and regular untinted glasses. The man who had taken my rifle away after I fell wounded and yelled out that I wanted to surrender was credited with making a "flying tackle" which "saved lives," and was hailed nationally as a hero.

Law students who readily admitted that they didn't know me very well nonetheless took the liberty of describing me as "a loner," "antisocial," and "off the deep end." A newspaper article devoted entirely to describing my life began with the words "Wendell Williamson had always been a little odd." A mentally ill drinking acquaintance I barely knew was quoted extensively, and this individual reported things about me which had no basis in reality but which were widely read and believed. For example, he said that I belonged to something called the "Conspiracy Club" which engaged in "endless discussions from all angles of conspiracy—the Vincent Foster case, the John F. Kennedy case, the Lincoln assassination and a few local cases, too." The same article said that at the law school I "couldn't get a close circle of friends." All these things were completely untrue.

However, it was from these newspaper articles that I learned who my victims were. The first man I killed had been a restaurant worker named Ralph Woodrow Walker, 42, and the second had been a UNC varsity lacrosse player named Kevin Eric Reichardt, 20. The police officer in the car I fired into was severely wounded in the hand, and her name was Demetrise Stephenson.

The man who tried to rescue Ms. Stephenson was a Chapel

Hill lawyer who I think was the biggest hero I saw that day because of the extent to which he endangered himself to save her. He never got much recognition that I am aware of, but he deserved it. There may have been another person with him, possibly another police officer, and if so they deserve recognition too (it was hard for me to see who was there, and even harder for me to remember it now).

Of course, I read none of this at the time it came out. For the first ten days I was in Central Prison, I stayed in the hospital part recovering from my gunshot wounds. I got a dose of the painkiller Percocet every four hours that I was awake, and spent most of my time in a dreamy sort of haze. The story of what I had done in Chapel Hill was all over the news during that time, and I watched on the television in our room as it came out bit by bit. My fellow inmate patients asked lots of questions about it, and I soon got tired of talking about the whole thing. It was clear that I had made a mistake in resorting to violence, since the police had not been afraid to shoot me after all, but all I could do now was make the best of it.

The inmate in the bed next to me seemed to be a nice person, and told me some of what he thought I should know about prison life. He had spent several years in prison himself, and was just returning on a parole violation. "I really dread it," he said. "All the bullshit, having to pretend to be tough all the time, people trying to take advantage of you, it's going to take an adjustment again. And I'll never leave here this time." He told me he had a terminal illness and was certain to die before he was released. A guard later told me it was AIDS.

This inmate was in the hospital being treated for a gunshot wound to the hand. He told me he had tried to commit suicide when he realized he was going back to prison, but had accidentally shot himself in the hand instead. It had been a hollow-point bullet, and his hand was pretty badly damaged. He was going to stay in the hospital as long as he possibly could, because it was better than being in the regular prison population.

In a bed across the room was another inmate who was being treated for a heart condition. He said he was being imprisoned for continuing to practice law after he had lost his license. That interested me, and he told me all about it. I told him I had been a law student, and he said he knew that. He had seen me on the news.

The three of us talked every day, and I enjoyed their company. Every morning at ten o'clock we would watch "Happy Days" and then "Laverne and Shirley" together, and laugh. It was odd to find something so prosaic here in this setting. I began to feel a little better about what lay ahead of me, if all the inmates were this friendly. The other patients in our room didn't say much. There was a dark-skinned black man across the room on the other side of the lawyer, a little old Hispanic man beside him, and a light-skinned black man beside me, who was being treated for a gun-shot wound to the hip.

One day the dark-skinned black man jumped up without warning, grabbed a chair, and beat the old Hispanic man bloody with it. The rest of us just lay there, waiting for him to attack one of us, but he just threw the chair aside and got back into his bed. After a while the inmate beside me asked him what he did that for, and he said the old Hispanic man wouldn't quit reading his thoughts. That sounded familiar, so I told the dark-skinned black man that that was the reason I had shot those people in Chapel Hill, because I had thought they wouldn't quit reading my thoughts. "And doing other stuff, too," I said.

"Like what?" asked the dark-skinned black man.

I told him some more of the stuff I had thought they were doing, and he recognized a lot of what I said as being things he had experienced. "I've got a voice in my head," he said. "It makes fun of me, like, for not having any money, and then it tells me what I should do to go make some money. It drives me crazy."

"Yeah," I said. "I had a voice like that, too. I called it 'that thing.' It was always telling me what I could or couldn't do, and making fun of me for stuff I couldn't help."

We talked about that stuff for a long time, and the dark-skinned black man finally ended up apologizing to the old Hispanic man for beating him bloody with a chair. The old Hispanic man just lay there in obvious terror, though. I'm not sure he even understood English.

Every night I took a shower, wrapping plastic garbage bags around my legs to keep the bandages from getting wet, wheeling to the shower room in a wheelchair, and sitting in a chair under the shower head. I couldn't stand up at all. It was painful to even try, and I always nearly fell over when I did.

Every day a nurse changed my bandages. Sometimes she would give a speech about what I had done to get myself into such a predicament, and said she hoped I would learn something from this experience. She asked me why I had done it, and when I told her she got really sarcastic and mean. She asked me where I got the rifle, and when I told her my father had bought it because it was like the one he had carried in World War II, she said, "You ought to be ashamed of yourself. For your father to go and fight for this country and then you go out and do something like this, I can just imagine what he thinks." I didn't feel ashamed, though, and only wished she could really understand what I had gone through so she would understand what I did. I didn't see it as any more wrong than what my father had done, given that I really couldn't have known what the right thing to do really was. It was my best try at doing the right thing, and I told her that, but she still didn't understand. "How could it be right to kill someone who has no way of defending himself?" she asked.

I explained about how they seemed to be able to exert painful control over my shoulder, but she still didn't understand. I don't think she believed me anyway, so I quit trying to explain my actions and just lay there and let her prattle on. It seemed to make her feel good to do that.

A doctor came to see me and took another X-ray of my left leg. It showed the metal rod and three screws the surgeon had used to put the bone back in place. The bone was still in pieces, and this doctor told me the smaller ones would eventually dissolve. The main part of the bone still looked a little crooked the way it had been fixed back, even after the surgery, and I suppose it still is. The doctor told me not to try to put any weight on that leg until he told me to, but to just use a wheelchair or crutches.

I got a number of visits from the outside while I was in the prison hospital. Dr. Warren came and performed a battery of psychological tests, and a psychiatrist named Dr. Bellard, whom my attorneys had retained, also came. Dr. Bellard had me tell the whole story in as much detail as I could remember, and asked many questions.

When I told Dr. Bellard about how it had seemed that other people seemed to be able to control my injured left shoulder at times, and seemed to be damaging it further simply by willing the socket apart, he said that phenomenon was called "tactile hallucinations," and that though rare, it was not unheard of. He said that such a thing could be caused by my mental illness. Giving it a name made me realize that I was not the first person to experience such horror, and also took away a lynchpin of my delusional ideas. Even though it hadn't seemed like it, it had all been my mind after all.

I always looked forward to my sessions with Drs. Warren and Bellard, not only because I liked them personally, but also because I believed what I told them was very important to my case and my future. I didn't embellish anything I told them, but just stuck to the plain, unvarnished truth, even when I knew this might hurt my case. I told them that I had known what I was doing, and had meant to do it, but I always made sure they understood my reasons. I thought it was very important that the entire story be known and understood for its own sake, because I knew it was a very unusual story. It was by far the most unusual and important thing that had ever happened to me, even before the shooting started. This was true whether I was telepathic or not.

I also made it clear that I had thought I would never have to tell this story, because I had thought everyone in the world already knew it.

These two doctors diagnosed me as suffering from paranoid schizophrenia.

My attorneys, James Williams and Kirk Osborn, also came to visit. I told them the same things I was telling Drs. Bellard and Warren. When I got to the part about believing I was doing the right thing by killing people, my attorneys smiled.

When they left after their first visit, I remained in the tiny visiting cell waiting for the guard to come and take me back up to my room. It was cold in there, and I was dressed only in a thin hospital gown and paper slippers. The hard metal seat became very uncomfortable, and my legs began to throb. I called out to the guard time and time again that I was finished and it was time to go, but still he didn't come. I think he was making me wait on purpose, because my attorneys must have told him when they left. I waited for more than an hour, constantly shifting positions from the seat to the table and back as best I could with my damaged legs. Finally I hit on the idea of singing to pass the time, and so I sang. Then the guard came, and we went back up to the hospital.

My singing must have been too much for him.

The food in prison was better than I had expected. The AIDS patient beside me told me the inmates cooked all their own food, and had to not only eat what they cooked but also contend with other inmates if the food wasn't good enough, so that kept the quality up. He also told me that working in the kitchen was one of the best jobs in the penitentiary, and might be something I would want to look into someday.

The only bad thing about the food was its constant sameness. After only a few days of eating it I noticed that even my skin was starting to smell like that food, and continued to smell that way for the rest of the time I was there.

On February 8, 1995, I was transferred to the Central Prison safekeeping psychiatric ward, Mental Health East. That morning a guard came carrying a rolled-up gold jumpsuit, a towel, and a set of sheets and pillowcase. He told me to put on the jumpsuit and carry the rest in a plastic bag. I did as he said, and followed him out of the hospital on my crutches. It was hard carrying the plastic bag and using the crutches at the same time, and as before, I had trouble keeping up. The guard often had to wait for me.

We went downstairs on an elevator, down a hall, and through a door into another hall. On one wall was a row of holding cells, and he put me in one and told me to wait. The inmate in the cell next to me wore a red jumpsuit, and asked me about my gold one. "That means safekeeping. What are you here for?" he asked.

"Murder," I said.

"Me too," he said. He pointed to his red jumpsuit and said, "This red means death row. Me, on death row. Can you believe that? I'll never leave here alive."

"That might be where I'm headed," I said. "What's it like?"

"It's just like safekeeping. Everybody else has jobs and makes money, but death row and safekeeping never do anything. We just sit there." He thought about it for a minute, and then said, "You look sort of familiar. Where would I have seen you before?"

"I've been on television a lot lately," I said.

"Oh, yeah, that's right," he said. "The Chapel Hill massacre. You got good lawyers?"

"I think so."

"Well if they're worth anything, they'll try to buy you some time. They'll put that trial off as long as possible. Are you scared of the death penalty?"

"No. I'm more scared of life in prison."

"Not me, man. I've been on death row for five years, and I'm scared to die. I'm saved, I've accepted Jesus Christ into my heart as my personal savior, and I know I'm going to heaven, but I'm still scared to die. There's nothing to do up there but sit around and think about it, you know?"

"Yeah, I can imagine."

"Have you accepted Jesus Christ?"

"No, I don't believe in God anymore."

"Well, you've got time. You'll come around."

A guard came and unlocked my cell door. "See you later," I said to the death row inmate. "Good luck."

"Yeah, good luck to you, too."

The guard led me across the hall into an office. A sergeant was there, and he said, "My name is Sergeant Rose. Pete Rose, just like the baseball player. You're going to be here a while in safekeeping. You know what that means?"

"Safekeeping?"

"Yeah."

"I guess it means I'm to be kept safely here until my trial."

"No, it just means you're to be kept here. Whether you're safe or not depends on you. We don't want any trouble out of you, and if anybody gives you any trouble, you come to me first. Got that?"

"Yes, Sergeant Rose."

He thanked me and I left. I had no intention of ever calling on Sergeant Rose to solve my problems for me, because I knew that sort of thing wouldn't be respected here, but still I was glad he had offered to help. He seemed nice enough, anyway.

The guard led me down a long corridor with windows that looked out on the exercise yard basketball courts, with chain-link fences all around topped by razor wire. Outside the fences were just more brick walls, too high to climb. He took me to an elevator and we rode up to the fourth floor, then we got out and he knocked on a door beside the elevator. A man inside nodded recognition, there was a buzzing sound, and the door next to it opened.

Inside was a day room with a grey concrete floor, several stainless-steel tables with stainless-steel seats welded to them, and a row of softer-looking vinyl seats around two walls. About a dozen lost-looking inmates in gold jumpsuits wandered around, some of them mumbling to themselves. I crutched my way inside behind the guard who had brought me.

A male nurse dressed in white came and took my weight and blood pressure, writing both down in a clipboard. He told me the meal times, and said I would be expected in the day room or I wouldn't eat. I said my leg was still giving me trouble, and asked if there was any way I could eat in my room instead. He said I could do that for the first 24 hours, and from then on I would have to eat in the day room with everyone else. He asked if I wanted to go to my bedroom right then, and I said I did.

He led me to the back of the day room and put a key in a lock. There was that whirring noise again, and the door opened. He led me down the hall to room 421, unlocked the door, and let me in. On the opposite wall was a bed. Beside the bed was a stainless steel toilet and sink with a polished metal mirror. The room was about 10 feet by 12, which was good enough for me right then. I thanked the nurse, lay down on the bed, and thought for a long time about my new situation. At some point since I had heard the police radios immediately after the shooting, I had already stopped believing that I even might be telepathic. I guess it was a combination of the antipsychotic Haldol, plus the coverage of the shooting, that had led me to see the truth at last. Nothing had turned out as I had really hoped, and now I was going to have to come to grips with the fact that I had killed two innocent men. It was really hard to comprehend.

That first day on Mental Health East I just spent in my room. Guards brought my meals to me, and I drifted in and out of sleep. I was afraid of the other inmates, because I figured they were criminally insane and therefore even more dangerous than those in the regular prison population. This must be the last circle of hell, I thought, and there was no telling how long I would have to stay.

The next morning the guards woke me up for breakfast and told me I had to come out into the day room. I was using crutches, and followed him back down the hall. Other inmates were moving that direction, rubbing the sleep out of their eyes.

When we got to the day room, most of the other inmates immediately went to the cigarette lighter affixed to the wall by the nurses' station. The nurses' station itself was completely closed off, but offered a window view of the entire day room. I had decided to quit smoking after the shooting, so I just sat down on one of the grey vinyl seats along the wall and waited for breakfast to come.

While I waited, I watched the other inmates with much trepidation. I expected to be attacked at any moment, as soon as they realized I was new. No one attacked me, though, and after a while I relaxed. Breakfast came about 45 minutes after we came into the day room, and there was some conversation while we were eating. I said nothing, though.

After breakfast a black inmate came over and introduced himself. I could tell that he was mentally retarded, but he seemed friendly, so we talked. He told me he was from the coast, and was about to be released. He didn't ask me what I was doing there, but he seemed concerned because I wasn't talking to anyone. I explained that I had some very serious charges to worry about. He said not to worry about it.

After we had talked for a while, he gave me his address at the coast and told me to come down when I got out and we would go dig oysters together. I still have his address.

I gradually got to know some of the inmates. They weren't all the violently insane people I had worried they might be. One of my favorites, and one of the first I met, was the canteen man. He had voluntarily taken the responsibility of collecting money and orders every day to send down to the canteen at breakfast time, and then to distribute the filled orders when they came back after lunch. He showed me the list of items available, and it included candy, instant coffee, tobacco, and toiletries. I told him I didn't have any money yet, and he gave me a candy bar out of his own pocket. "Somebody gave me one when I first got here and didn't have any money," he said, "so maybe you can do somebody else the same favor when you can. There really are some nice people here." I appreciated that candy bar so much that since then, wherever I have been, I have always made it a point to be generous with new arrivals, because of the kindness the canteen man had shown me when I first arrived at Mental Health East.

I asked the canteen man how long he had been there, and he said since November 1994. "That was when I killed my wife," he said.

I asked what happened, and he said he didn't want to talk about it. "I could tell you all about it," he said, "but then after a while I would just be an emotional wreck because of having to talk about it. I'm still really upset about what happened."

I said I understood, and from that time on asked him no questions about what had happened unless he voluntarily brought it up, which he did from time to time. I could tell it was always on his mind, though. He later told me that he had left behind three small children who would probably have to be put up for adoption. "I should have divorced her," he said, "but I didn't want to leave those kids." He was really torn up about everything—the beautiful wife he had loved who was now dead because of him, the three children who would remember little of their real parents, his own hopeless situation. I came to have a lot of respect for the canteen man, but I always felt sorry for him, too. He was in the psychiatric unit because he was bipolar (which used to be called "manic depressive"), and all of his woes just made his illness worse.

Another inmate I really liked was there because he had killed the man who had molested his young son. He told me his son had been terribly upset about being molested, that he was afraid of the man, and that the inmate had felt like he had to do something about it. He said he didn't go to the man's house intending to kill him, but that that was what ended up happening. He said most people in his home county were on his side, and he hoped to get his murder charge reduced to voluntary manslaughter.

"He doesn't deserve even that," said the canteen man. "He deserves the Congressional Medal of Honor."

The inmate who had killed the man who had molested his son asked me what I was charged with, and I told him. When I mentioned Chapel Hill, it rang a bell. "Oh yeah, I remember hearing about that," he said. Then he said something that really stuck with me: "Did you ever notice that the nicest people you meet in prison are the killers?"

I hadn't met enough killers at that time to be able to agree or disagree with him, but since then I have, and I have to agree with what he said. I've met dozens of killers, and nearly all of them have been people I could get along with easily. Most of them just got pushed by circumstances into doing something anyone might do in the same situation, and most of the killers I met struck me as people who would never kill again, even if they got the chance. Few of the ones I met were the monsters the news media made them out to be, but most of them will spend the rest of their lives behind bars. I understand why it has to be that way, but it's still too bad.

About this time I discovered that I could walk without crutches. One day a guard came and took me to see an orthopedic doctor about my legs, and I walked down there without the crutches. The doctor was aghast. He told me he wanted me on crutches or in a wheelchair until he said otherwise, or I would risk doing permanent damage to my left leg. The nurse upstairs, Mr. Hirsch, wouldn't let me keep crutches in the day room because he said they might be used as weapons, so I put in a request for a wheelchair.

A guard brought the wheelchair up that night. It's my wheelchair birthday, I thought morosely, remembering something the female voices used to say. For my next ten weeks in the prison, I remained in that wheelchair. In a way it was better that way, because it had a soft seat and I didn't have to sit on the hard metal stools around the tables in the day room.

When Annetta and I were still dating, she and her family had taught me to play spades. I was still a novice at the game when I arrived at Central Prison, but I quickly discovered that it was a major pastime behind prison walls, and I started playing again. Every day there would be spades games. Over the next few months I played a lot, and gradually developed a system of bidding my hand that is nearly foolproof. I still use it, and call it my "Central Prison system."

When I wasn't playing spades, I read. There was a small book-shelf in the day room, and I found "Baa Baa Black Sheep," the story of a famous World War II Marine fighter squadron. It was written by the squadron commander, Major Gregory Boyington, who in 1944 was shot down and captured by the Japanese. He spent the next year and a half in a Japanese prisoner of war camp, and his strategies for coping with confinement I found to be use-ful.

While I was still reading that book, I told Dr. Bellard what I was reading, and he said that his father had been a pilot in the Black Sheep squadron. "Yeah, he knew all those guys," Dr. Bellard said. I was fascinated. He promised to someday wear his Black Sheep leather jacket to show me.

Gradually I learned about life in a maximum-security peniten-tiary. We were totally sealed off from the outside. There was no telephone. No packages could be received from anywhere, unless they were books, and then they had to be sent directly from the publisher. Your own family couldn't send any you already owned. The only exception to the no-packages rule was for a few weeks at Christmas, and then everything was closely searched. All mail was searched, and no one could send stamps.

A guard explained this rule to me. "Some people were real joke-sters," he said. "They started putting LSD on stamps."

Those rules applied to the entire penitentiary. There were other rules which applied only to mental patients, such as no dental floss, for fear we might try to hang ourselves with it. We also weren't allowed to smoke in our bedrooms, for fear that we might try to set the place on fire.

There was no lying down in the day room, and no going to the bedroom except at appointed times, which came every two or three hours. Once you were in your bedroom, you had to stay there until the next appointed time, two or three hours away, and you weren't allowed to bang on your door while you were there. Many inmates ignored this last rule, and it was hard to sleep even at night because of all the banging and screaming by the deranged. It was like trying to sleep in a bus station, with the constant commotion, people coming and going, lights turning on and off, and so on. I eventually got used to it, though, and came to think of the place as home.

Sometimes the inmates would sing. Gospel music was common, and sometimes they would achieve beautiful harmonies. Every once in a while an inmate would preach a sermon, which was always entertaining to listen to. Also, some of the inmates were better at banging in rhythm than others, and when the best drummers started I kind of enjoyed listening to them. Sometimes a drumming session would last all night, with singing, preaching, screaming, and talking back and forth about every subject imaginable.

One day after I had been there a while but before my parents sent me any money, the guards brought everyone a big bag of homemade cookies. They said they had been baked by a local church. I really appreciated that gift because I was going around hungry most of the time, and it made me want to prove myself worthy of those churchgoers' generosity. It made me want to show kindness, too.

The one vice we were allowed was smoking. After a while I got tired of denying myself this pleasure, and one evening I asked someone for a cigarette. It tasted great. As soon as my money came I ordered a carton of Marlboros, and have smoked every day since. I smoke Camel Lights now, though, because that was my brand before I got locked up. Central Prison just didn't sell Camel Lights at the canteen, and Marlboros were close enough.

During this time more and more was coming out in the news about my history of mental illness. The other inmates took all of this in and told me everything would work out for me. "They won't convict you," one said. "You'll do maybe two to five years, tops." All of this didn't make me feel any better, though. It hadn't forced people to admit that I was telepathic, because I really wasn't telepathic in the first place, and now two innocent men were dead because of what I viewed as nothing more than my own hard-headedness. I didn't want to avoid responsibility for my actions. I didn't see that as manful. I wanted the death penalty, and I told them so.

"You're crazy, man," one said.

"That's the point, isn't it?" said another. "He's crazy, and that's why he's going to get off."

I didn't want to "get off." What I really wanted wasn't going to happen, and I thought the next best thing would be for me to accept the punishment I thought I had coming to me, and die for what I had done. After all, I had killed people with the full knowledge that I might be mentally ill and not telepathic. It was just the chance that I was telepathic, and that we were all in danger as a result, that had made me do it. I had been wrong, and the only truly just solution would be for me to go the same way as my victims.

Ideally, I didn't think I really deserved to die, because I had done my best. However, my victims hadn't deserved to die, either. It just wasn't an ideal universe, and I felt like most people would feel better about the whole thing if I were executed, and executed soon. That was what I would work toward.

At my attorneys' next visit, I told them through the visiting room plexiglas that I didn't want to challenge the death penalty. I told them I thought the death penalty would be the solution most agreeable to everyone.

My attorneys wouldn't hear of it. They said that my feelings might raise the question of my competency to stand trial, and that would just mean a very long stay in a mental hospital. "If you want to stay in a mental hospital a long time, you just keep talking like you want to die," Kirk Osborn said. He left me with the impression that I would probably spend less time in a mental hospital if I was acquitted by reason of insanity than I would on death row if I were convicted and sentenced to die.

Dr. Bellard said the same thing later, so I finally had to give up on the idea of having any control over what the system did with me. My fate was now beyond my control.

Meanwhile, the other inmates tried to sympathize with me. "It's okay," they would say. "You didn't know what you were doing," they would say, even though I still believed I had known what I was doing. "You couldn't control yourself," they would say, even though I had been able to control myself. "You snapped," they would say, or "You just went off," or "You just lost it," even though I didn't think any of these phrases accurately described what had really happened. It had been a carefully planned, calculated move made with full awareness of the risks, at least as I saw them. I had simply overestimated some of the risks I saw in assuming I was mentally ill and therefore in need of medication.

At least that's how I was feeling at the time of the shooting. Now, as I read back over this, I can only think God, how could I have been so stupid? And there is no answer.

My parents came to visit. We met in the usual visiting room, separated by plexiglas. I felt self-conscious in my gold jumpsuit. They asked how I was doing, and I told them I was fine. They asked about my gunshot wounds, and I showed them my scars.

My father told me my name had been mentioned by Ted Koppel on the night of the shooting, that some of his army buddies had heard the news from as far away as Arizona, and that the man who had taken my rifle away had been awarded a silver medal for heroism. I asked if the people I had seen trying to rescue the wounded police officer from her car while I was shooting at them had gotten any recognition, and he said no. I said I thought they deserved it more than the man who had taken my rifle away, because I had already given up by the time he did that.

We visited for a while, and then they put some money in my account and left. I went back to my cellblock happy that they had come, but I still felt badly about causing them so much worry.

During one session with my attorneys, Kirk Osborn said that people saw in what I had done "everything that's wrong with society." I didn't see what my situation had to do with anything that's going on in society. He also told me he was going to have to educate the trial jury about paranoid schizophrenia. "We're going to have to show them that you lived in a different moral universe from the rest of us," he said.

I didn't think I had been in a different moral universe at all. If those people had really been up to what I thought they were up to, it wouldn't have been moral to allow them to get away with it, in anybody's "moral universe." I told him what I thought, but he didn't seem to understand. After a while I decided to just let him run my defense however he wanted to, and I would just answer his questions or keep quiet. It was frustrating that no one understood my point of view, but there really wasn't anything I could do about it.

One day Dr. Bellard said, "I don't think you're going to end up in prison, Wendell."

I asked him where he thought I would end up, and he said in a mental hospital. "It won't be quite as bad," he said, "though at first it will be just as confining."

I asked him how long he thought I would be in the mental hospital, and he said I had to worry about my trial first, which might still be as much as a year away. After that I would probably go to a mental hospital for at least a few weeks, and then I would have a commitment hearing. "Will you have a snowball's chance of getting out of the hospital at that first hearing?" he asked rhetorically. "Probably not. After that there will be periodic hearings, and if you give them no reason to hold you, your chances will improve with each one. What you need to prove is that you are either no longer mentally ill, which will be impossible because paranoid schizophrenia is a chronic illness which will always require that you take medication, or that you are no longer dangerous, which can only be proven by a long period of not being dangerous."

"I'm not dangerous now. When do you think they'll release me?" I asked.

"I don't know," he said. "Maybe after a year. Maybe," he said, emphasizing the last "maybe." "It's all going to be up to you. I know that it will be very tempting to start thinking that this is all beyond your control and just give up, but it really isn't. You'll need to go to all your activities, show no signs of continuing psychosis or violent tendencies, and so on. But your problems won't be over when you leave there. You may be able to go somewhere else and live a relatively normal life, or you may not."

That was bad news. I didn't want to spend the next two years locked up, and I wanted to be able to live a normal life when I left. I didn't think these wants were unreasonable. I had thought what I had done was an honorable thing, and I had just been honestly mistaken. It wasn't like I was ever going to do something like that again.

I began having long hours of black depression. As if it wasn't bad enough that I had shot and killed or wounded several completely innocent people, which was worse than anything I had ever dealt with, but now it looked like my life was forever going to be ruined because of it. Also, the canteen man didn't think I would be released in as little as two years, despite what Dr. Bellard had said. "Maybe six or seven," said the canteen man. "And I think that's pretty reasonable, considering what you did."

I didn't think it was so reasonable. My actions had in no way been a product of evil intent. If someone had killed two people in self-defense, which is what I had thought I was doing, then they wouldn't have to spend any time at all in prison or in a mental hospital. I failed to see the difference between such a person's level of fault and mine. In fact, killing two people just to save your own neck is less justifiable than killing two people to save the world, if that's what you're really trying to do. I could see how someone like me might have to prove that he's not going to make a similar mistake again, but surely it wouldn't take years to do that. I thought that the effectiveness of my psychotropic medication should be enough proof. I should just have to prove that I would continue to take the medication after I left, which I would. I, more than anyone, didn't want to make the same mistake again.

I found an inmate from New Jersey who was there for stealing a truck and joyriding. He had spent ten years in a mental hospital there, so I began pumping him for information about life in such a facility. He said it was a lot better than our situation in Central Prison. "The people really care about you in a mental hospital," he said. "I mean, life isn't the greatest when you're there, but it's a lot better than this. These people don't care at all about what happens to us."

To see if he was right, I asked a staff member, Mr. Hirsch, one night while he was changing my bandages what he thought would happen to me. Mr. Hirsch said I would have to seriously adjust my expectations in life. Even if I should happen to be acquitted at trial, which he didn't think would happen, I would never be able to do the things I would have been able to do if I hadn't turned violent.

February became March, and the boredom began to get to me. Old inmates left and new ones arrived. I always tried to be especially nice to the new arrivals just like the canteen man had been with me, and I made three new friends. All of them were years younger than me.

One was only sixteen. He had a shaved head, and he told me he was charged with robbing a convenience store and shooting the man behind the cash register. The man had survived, and now all his relatives wanted to kill the sixteen-year-old. "I don't know why I even did it," he said. "I had plenty of money in my pockets, but somebody said let's go do it, so I went along. We really roughed up the old man, too, beating him up and kicking him after we shot him. They got the whole thing on videotape. How much time do you think I'll get?"

I didn't know.

The other two young inmates were less violent. One was seventeen, and he was there on a drug violation of some sort. He was really interested to learn I was there for murder, and wanted to know what it was like to kill someone. "I've been thinking about killing this guy, too. I bet it feels pretty good, doesn't it?"

I said it didn't feel good at all, and told him he'd better not do something like that.

There was a twenty-year-old who was there for some long and involved transaction that included trading several pounds of marijuana for a pair of stolen jet skis, plus breaking and entering, larceny, and a few other things. "All non-violent," he said. "How much time do you think I'll get?"

Again, I didn't know. People thought that just because I'd been to law school that I knew everything and could give them good legal advice about their own problems, when really I hadn't learned that much criminal law when I was in school, and I usually found that other inmates knew more about that kind of stuff than I did. I always told them that I was mentally ill the whole time I was in law school, and hadn't learned as much as I should have. Most of them thought I was faking it, but that didn't bother them. They said they would fake it too if they were facing murder charges. In fact, a few wanted advice on how to fake paranoid schizophrenia. I never gave out that kind of advice.

I also got to know an inmate who had been there for a while. I had arrived at Mental Health East at the start of the Islamic holy month of Ramadan, and I noticed that he didn't eat with the rest of us during the day, so I guessed that he was a Muslim. I asked him about it, and he seemed pleased that I took an interest. We talked about Christian and Muslim views of God, spirituality, and the afterlife, and he showed me his Koran. It was a beautiful book, a hardcover inlaid with gold, and it read from back to front. Its title I believe was spelled "Quo'ran," or something close to that. It had an index, and I looked up various subjects to see what it said about each. For example, I looked up "sex and marriage," and it said that a man may enter a woman in any way, as long as it is in the vagina. A man who cannot afford to support a wife must abstain from marriage until he can afford to do so. There were other useful tidbits like that, and I thought the whole thing was interesting.

This particular inmate was accused of a horrible crime, and at first denied having done it, but later confided to me that he had in fact done it. He said he was a paranoid schizophrenic, and that the voices he was hearing had him so confused that he acted on what they told him to do. He felt terrible remorse afterward, and was very afraid of what the penal system would do to him. I sympathized, and we talked for a long time about mental illness, crime, punishment, and what is truly just. He remained my friend for the rest of the time I was in Central Prison.

Of course, there were other inmates whose behavior was such that I didn't want to approach them. There were occasional violent outbursts, and I always felt that someone could get badly hurt at any time. No one ever accosted me, however, and in fact I never saw an argument escalate beyond what would happen on the outside. Most of us realized that we were just going to have to get along with each other because we didn't have any choice, and it worked out pretty well.

"This is the romper room," said the canteen man one day. "It's a lot worse in regular population."

One day the enormity of my situation suddenly hit me, and I knew I was about to start crying. I put out my cigarette, went to the bathroom and closed the door behind me, and broke down in sobs. Everything that there was to cry about, my lost future, my present circumstances, and the fact that I had killed and wounded people who hadn't deserved it at all, it all came out. I stayed in the bathroom about an hour, then dried my eyes, washed my face, and went back into the day room as if nothing had happened.

I was to have many more crying spells over the following months. They usually came at night as I lay in my bed, when I could be alone. Only once did another inmate say anything about it, and he only said, "Whatever it is that's bothering you, I want you to know that it's going to be all right." I didn't think so, but I didn't want to talk about it, either.

Late in March the canteen man found out that he would soon be in the regular population. His attorney had advised that he take a guilty plea on one count of second-degree murder. He agreed, and one day in early April he was gone. The judge had given him a sentence of life without possibility of parole. I was very sad to see him go, for he had been such a good friend that it was hard to think of him having to face life without any real hope. I missed him terribly, and began writing him letters. We still keep in contact by mail.

With him gone, I became the new canteen man. For several days I took orders, collected money, and distributed goodies. For this I was paid one candy bar a day. Someone else wanted the job, though, and so I let them have it because they couldn't afford to buy a candy bar every day on their own. Besides that, the job required that I get up for breakfast every morning so I could give the guards the orders and the money for that day, and I was finding it better for my peace of mind to just sleep through breakfast. Mornings were just too depressing. In fact, I soon began sleeping through lunch, too, and not coming out into the day room until midafternoon. I went around hungry a lot because of that, but it was better than having to face the day all day long, and every day.

Another new inmate came in. He told me he had been a career Marine, and that the sheriff's department in his county was suspicious of him because he kept a lot of weapons around the house and was an explosives expert. He said one day they got a search warrant and went through his house, taking a number of his personal belongings including and address book that listed all of his old buddies from the Marines. He had argued with the deputies, ended up getting into a fight with them, and got locked up on an assault charge. I don't remember how he got from his county jail to the state penitentiary, but somehow he had. He didn't expect to be there long.

He was interesting to talk to. He told me he had fought in Vietnam (he had carried an M-14), and that he had been awarded the Navy Cross. He had just completed a book about his experiences and was in the process of getting it published when he got locked up. This was not the first time he had been in prison, but the time before his conviction had been overturned on appeal. I told him about my situation, and he said not to expect to be released before at least three or four years had passed. "And that would be with flying colors," he said. He had seen stories like mine before, he said. "Just promise me one thing," he said. "When you do get out, don't play with guns any more."

I promised.

On April 19 we watched the news as the story of the Oklahoma City bombing unfolded. "That sounds like something you'd do, Wendell," said one inmate. I was really offended. To me, bombing innocent people and then trying to get away is a very cowardly act. What I had done had put my life on the line, too. I had reasoned that if I was truly killing innocent people, then I would be killed too. The only way I would survive unscathed was if I was truly the telepath I had thought I was, and that in turn would have meant that the people I had killed hadn't been innocent at all. In other words, I would only get away with what I had done if it was truly the right thing to do. Whoever had bombed the federal building in Oklahoma had tried to get away with it whether the people he had killed were innocent or not.

I tried to explain this, but the inmate didn't understand. The more I explained, the less he understood, so I finally quit trying. It was really irritating, though, to think there were other people who would probably equate what I did with any act of senseless violence. They just didn't understand, and yet they were in a position to really mess my life up.

Late in April I was scheduled to go back to Orange County, North Carolina for my arraignment. After that I was to go to Dorothea Dix mental hospital for my pretrial evaluation. Dr. Bellard explained that my pretrial evaluation would address two questions: first, whether or not I was competent to proceed to trial, and second, whether or not I was to be deemed criminally responsible for my acts. He, too, would be evaluating me on both questions. He asked if I understood the nature of the charges against me, and how I planned to assist my attorneys in preparing a defense.

I told him that I understood the charges and what they were, and that I planned to assist the attorneys in preparing a defense by telling them the truth about my state of mind at the time of the shooting. I knew that if I wasn't able to understand and do these things, that I would be considered incompetent to stand trial. That would mean a lengthy stay in a mental hospital, and would probably prolong my period of confinement, so I was eager to be found competent and get the trial over with so I could begin working on proving that I was no longer dangerous.

Dr. Bellard said he considered me "super-competent" to stand trial, especially since I had been to law school, but that my attorneys wanted him to be absolutely certain. He asked me questions about what would happen at trial, who the judge was and what he was to do, who the district attorney was and what he was to attempt to prove, and the role of the jury. I knew all of this, and explained it in detail. He seemed satisfied with my answers, and told me that his recommendation would be that I was competent to proceed to trial, but that I was not criminally responsible for my actions because I satisfied what is called the "M'Naghten rule" of insanity.

The M'Naghten rule says essentially that a person is legally insane, and therefore not criminally responsible for his actions, if he has a mental disease or defect of reason which causes him to either not be able to control his actions, or not be able to appreciate the wrongfulness of those actions. It is the strictest insanity rule in common usage in the United States. In other words, it is the one which makes it most difficult to gain an acquittal. Dr. Bellard deemed me to satisfy it because he had diagnosed me as being paranoid schizophrenic, which satisfies the "mental disease or defect" element of the test, and because this condition had caused me to believe that my actions were morally right, which satisfies the second element. It was not necessary that the disease also prevent me from being able to control my actions, because I satisfied the other prong of the test, the "unable to appreciate wrongfulness" part. This was good for me, because I had in fact been able to control my actions.

I understood all of this. I had studied it in law school. I had hoped it would never have to be applied to me, however, because I was hoping that I wasn't really mentally ill. In fact, I had tried before the shooting to sabotage any possible use of the insanity defense by telling people I knew how to get away with killing someone, so long as you established your insanity beforehand. I was hoping at the time that this little hint would warn people that

I was planning to kill, so that they would admit I was telepathic and so save themselves.

My lawyers later heard rumors that I had made statements to that effect before the shooting, and they were very alarmed. They said it would be potentially disastrous to my case if testimony like that went before the jury. They asked me if I had ever made statements like that and why, and at the time they asked me this I had forgotten about ever having made the statements, so I denied it. I remember it now, though, and if I had remembered it then I would have told my attorneys what I just told you, that I made those statements both to sabotage any possible use of the insanity defense so I could prove that the state was still afraid to kill me, and also to warn people that I was serious and that they had better admit I was telepathic before somebody got hurt or killed. I hadn't wanted to be able to take advantage of the insanity defense because I had wanted to give the state every reason to have me executed, so that I could show that they were still afraid to do it. This, I thought, would prove at least that I was being considered a very special case, and so would lend credence to my claim that I was telepathic.

I could have still done all this, but I now no longer believed I was telepathic, so I saw no sense in making an ass of myself at trial. I decided to just let the defense play out however it was going to, and hope that someday I could explain what my plan had been so that people could understand.

On the evening before my arraignment, a female guard came and got me. "Let's blow this popsicle stand," she said. I followed her out of Mental Health East on my crutches, down the elevator, and through the long corridors leading to the entrance of the prison.

We finally came to the place where I had been strip-searched that day in January that now seemed so long ago. There was a deputy sheriff from Orange County waiting for me there. They processed me out, and then he led me outside to his car. It was the first time I had been outside the prison in three months, and after we left the last gate behind I stared in wonder at the roads, the cars, the people, all just as I had left it. They were all peaceably going about their business, and it made me sad to think that I might never be one of them, just going peaceably about mine.

We arrived at the Hillsborough jail and the deputies brought me inside. I was dressed in the castoff clothes the hospital had given me to wear to Central Prison three months earlier, which had been kept in a locker for me at the prison. The deputies gave me an orange jumpsuit to wear, with orange sandals, and led me to a holding cell just across the hall from an office. They didn't want me housed with other prisoners, so I spent the night in the holding cell. After a while they fed me supper, which was a welcome change from the Central Prison food. After that I just sat there for hours, smoking one cigarette after another. When it came time to go to sleep, I asked for another blanket because it was very cold in the cell, and they brought me one.

The next morning they woke me up, fed me breakfast, and told me my case would come up early. I smoked a few more cigarettes, and then they gave me the civilian clothes I had worn the day before. I put these on in the presence of two deputies, who gave me a steel leg brace that I had to wear to keep me from trying to escape. The leg brace is a long steel bar that runs inside one's pants along the outside of the leg and fastens around the leg with velcro straps. It has a hinge at the knee and can be unlocked with a lever when one walks or sits down.

They then led me out of the jail toward the courthouse. I was still on my crutches and slowed down even more by the leg brace. All around me, dogwoods were blooming in the warm April morning. It was a beautiful sight after so much greyness in the prison, and I wondered if I would ever see anything like it again. It was sad to think that if things had been different, I might have soon been working as a lawyer in such a beautiful place. This is where I really belong, I thought, not in prison.

As we neared the courthouse across the street, I saw the press.

There were dozens of reporters and cameramen filming my approach. They shouted questions at me, but I said nothing. My attorneys had told me just to ignore the press. It was one of the most embarrassing situations of my life.

Inside the courthouse I saw many well-dressed people. They all stared as I entered surrounded by my entourage of law-enforcement personnel. We went upstairs in an elevator, and then they led me into the courtroom.

There were cameras inside the courtroom, too. Everything was hushed as I was led to my seat at the defense counsel table. James Williams and Kirk Osborn were waiting for me there, and Kirk whispered a few words of encouragement to me before the judge entered.

Judge Gordon Battle then came into the courtroom, and we all rose until he sat down. He went over a few preliminary matters, and then turned to my case. I don't remember much of what followed, except that when it came time for me to enter my pleas, they read each of the fifteen felony counts separately, and to each one James Williams replied, "Not guilty, and not guilty by reason of insanity." There were gasps behind me, and murmurs. After the pleas were entered, Judge Battle ordered that I be sent to Dorothea Dix Hospital for an evaluation period not to exceed sixty days.

When it was over, a deputy sheriff led me out of the courtroom and down a flight of stairs. Outside the press came at me again, and still I said nothing. We went to a sheriff's car, and as we were leaving the parking lot I saw a young woman who one of the deputies said was a family member of one of the victims. As our car passed her, she just kept shaking her head and saying, "No, no, no." I felt sick.

We drove back to Raleigh while the deputies made small talk with me. They seemed nice, and didn't ask anything about the case. They asked about what it was like for me in the prison, and I told them so far, so good. They said it was too bad I was in so much trouble, but that it was spilt milk now. I agreed.

We arrived at Dorothea Dix, which is just across Western Boulevard from Central Prison. We wound along a few roads on the hospital grounds, and I watched the patients I saw wandering around. Maybe I'll be one of them someday, I thought.

At last we came to a building which had a large exercise yard enclosed by two layers of chain link fences topped by razor wire. This was the forensic psychiatry division, better known as the Spruill Building. We went inside, and I was led to yet another holding cell. I sat down, and the deputies said goodbye and left. I watched through the bars as people came and went. None of them was dressed in any kind of uniform, which was strange to me after my months at the prison, where nearly everyone wears a uniform or a jumpsuit.

After a while someone came and let me out of the cell. He led me down a hall, through some barred gates, and up a flight of stairs. I couldn't climb the stairs with my crutches, so I just handed them to him and climbed them anyway. "You don't need crutches," he said.

"Yes I do," I said. "My doctor told me I had to use them until he says so."

"No you don't," he said. "You're cured."

Upstairs he led me to a doctor's office. Inside was a young Asian doctor who asked me why I was there. I told him the whole story, which he wrote down. He asked many questions and wrote down my answers. When he was finished he called for a health-care technician, and when the tech came we went through some more barred gates and onto a long hall. Many patients were walking up and down that hall. The tech led me to a closet, where he handed me a pair of state pants, a state shirt, socks, and underwear. I went to a bathroom and put these on. Then he led me down the hall to a day room which, like the hall, was very crowded. I found a nice soft seat and sat down. It was very comfortable after the hard metal seats of Central Prison.

Outside the window I could see a huge maple tree with all its light-green spring leaves. It reminded me of a Van Gogh painting, and I wondered if Vincent Van Gogh had been similarly inspired by something he saw from the windows of a mental hospital. It seemed that he had.

I wanted a cigarette, but they had explained to me that no smoking was allowed inside the building, and that every two hours they would let me smoke outside on a screened-in porch. I watched the clock until the next smoke break, and then smoked four cigarettes in the twenty minutes I was allowed. While I was smoking I tentatively got to know some of the other patients. All of them were in trouble with the law, and many of them seemed very mentally ill.

Soon after we came back inside, I wanted another cigarette, so I started watching the clock again. I was to spend most of my sixty days there just waiting for the next cigarette break.

At supper time we all went downstairs into the basement, where there was a room with two long rows of tables with blue vinyl tablecloths. We lined up and they handed out trays, with the patients on special diets being served first. The food wasn't as good as the prison food had been, but I ate some of it anyway.

After supper we all went out into the exercise yard. The techs gave us each our pack of cigarettes, and we were allowed to smoke as many as we wanted for the next two hours or so. My mood improved, and I got to know some of the other patients. The one I liked the best had been sent there by his mother. He was about twenty years old, and was accused of statutory rape because he had had sex with his fourteen-year-old fiancée, or so he said. He showed me her picture and said he was going to marry her when he got out. I said she was very pretty, which she was, and wished them luck. We talked for a long time, and he didn't strike me as the criminal type or mentally ill. He even loaned me a novel to read, which was a real bonus.

Some of the patients started a basketball game, but I didn't join them because I didn't want to push my left leg. I just sat on a concrete picnic table and smoked and talked to other patients to learn as much as I could about life in the Spruill Building. We stayed outside until the sun went down, and then we went back inside, turning in our cigarette packs as we entered. Mine was noticeably thinner.

Upstairs we went to the vending machines, where I got two cups of real coffee. Then we were handed peanut butter sandwiches and milk, which were better than the supper had been. None of these things had been available at the prison.

I was on the ten o'clock news that night, and my new friends suddenly realized who I was. Some asked questions, some wanted autographs (which I didn't give), and everyone was awed. My anonymity was gone.

Over the next few weeks I underwent a grueling series of psychological tests. Nearly everything I had seen before, and my answers didn't change much. My attorneys told me to answer the questions on the MMPI as I would have answered them at the time of the shooting, so I said I heard voices in my head, that I believed other people were watching me, and so on. There was a test which required that I finish uncompleted sentences, such as "This place (blank)," or "Men (blank)." I had to once again interpret inkblots, tell stories about pictures, and tell what it means when we say that a rolling stone gathers no moss or that people in glass houses shouldn't throw stones. I still didn't know how far it was from New York to Paris, but apparently I needed to find out.

During this time I still had a habit of sleeping until after lunch, and it bothered me greatly to be dragged out of bed early in the mornings to take these tests. I never felt that I was at my best at such an hour, and it was difficult to come up with responses to the tests that I was satisfied with. Even more important, sometimes the doctors would ask again about what had led up to the shooting, and I became very tired of telling the same story over and over. Sometimes I would omit important things that I simply forgot about, and sometimes I remembered new things which brought on renewed barrages of questions. All I could think about was sleep.

I told my staff psychiatrist about this, and she diagnosed me as suffering from depression. It was true that I was depressed, but it was situational depression and could be corrected only with a change for the better in my life situation, which I didn't foresee happening. No one could take away what had already happened. Nevertheless the doctor prescribed the antidepressant Zoloft, which I took, even though it upset my stomach. One of my most enduring memories of that period at the Spruill Building is of lying in bed every day, unwilling to get up and face the trials of my new existence, and suffering from an upset stomach.

One thing that the doctors really concentrated on was whether I had suffered from an unhappy childhood or problems with my family. They seemed to think that only a person who grew up mal-adjusted could do such a monstrous thing as what I had done. No matter how many times I told the story of what had led me to kill, they still seemed determined to put their own interpretation of my psychological deficiencies on the whole thing. They would ask if I had felt I was a failure in life, if I had had trouble making friends and keeping them, and that sort of thing. They seemed very reluctant, if not outright unwilling, to see this as I did—that under the right circumstances, even a well-adjusted person can believe he has a duty to kill others because of the threat they pose.

I suppose that some people reading this will wonder how I could think I was well-adjusted when I thought these people I had killed had posed a threat they didn't really pose, but to these people I ask, how does a person adjust well to a phenomenon such as that which I was experiencing? How can one know the truth under such circumstances? You can only try to do the best thing, and no one should expect anything more. I believe that anyone who continues to try to do the right thing even under the most adverse of conditions is well-adjusted. I will always believe that, no matter what happens to me.

My family came to visit me, and they brought Camel Light

cigarettes because the Central Prison rules on packages didn't apply at the Spruill Building. I still felt embarrassed to be with them because I knew they couldn't understand what had happened, but they still had faith in me. That must have been very difficult for them.

After a few weeks I met with Dr. Rollins, the head of the forensic psychiatry division. My attorneys attended this meeting. Dr. Rollins asked what had led me into the situation in which I now found myself, and I told him as much as I could remember. He asked questions, which I answered. The meeting was fairly brief, and at the end he asked if I had anything to add. I said I was very sorry things had gone as far as they had, and I meant it. Just because I still felt I had done my best to do the right thing didn't change my sorrow over having killed and wounded people who had turned out to be completely innocent.

My attorneys diligently took notes during this meeting, but said little. "This is your meeting," Kirk Osborn explained.

One of the worst things about being in the Spruill Building, aside from the overcrowding and occasional fights that it brought on, was that there were no toilets in our rooms like there had been at the prison. We were locked in our rooms every night, and if we had to go to the bathroom, we had to knock on our doors to be let out. It usually took the technicians a while to answer, and there's nothing worse than waking up in the middle of the night needing to use the bathroom and then having to wait fifteen or twenty minutes for someone to come and let you. All night long there would be people standing there knocking and begging to be allowed to go to the bathroom.

May of 1995 passed sadly for me. I remember lying in the grass out in the exercise yard, too sleepy and depressed to get up and move around like most of the other patients were doing. My 27th birthday came and went, and I wanted only to die. I wanted someone to just drive up to the fence, pull out a rifle, and shoot me to death. I thought this would in a sense be fair, and in a sense not. I supposed that which sense was more important would depend on who you asked. I personally didn't care much, but I was leaning toward the suicidal end of the spectrum. I still cursed God for putting me into the position that had led me here, but I felt empty because I couldn't believe there was even a God there to listen.

I still met new people, but they made little impression. By this time I had heard it all, every conceivable twist on every imaginable crime. The one common thread was that everyone had some kind of mental problem. In fact, thinking back on that time there are only a few people I can even remember. One was an alcoholic who was accused of getting drunk, attempting to rape a woman, and then shooting her in the leg. He denied everything except the part about getting drunk. He seemed very morose about his legal problems, but he seemed to like my company, so I tolerated him.

On the night before he went back to his county jail to await trial, it rained. We were out on the porch smoking cigarettes, and he stuck his hand out into the warm raindrops falling. "That may be the last time I get to feel rain for a very long time," he said. I wonder what ever became of him.

Another friend I made was a soft-spoken Christian. Even though I no longer believed in God I still liked his attitude. He was there because when he discovered his wife was cheating on him with five other men, he drove to one of their homes, knocked on the door, and when the man answered, shot him dead. He said he knew it wasn't the Christian thing to do. He said he was an emotional basket case both before and after the shooting, especially since he had such high moral standards for himself and his wife. He said he expected to go to prison, and while he was there he hoped to write a book about the decline of the American family. He and I talked a lot about philosophy, religion, and morality. One thing I really liked about him was that even though he really did seem to have high moral standards, and even though he didn't understand what had led me to kill, he still didn't try to judge me for what I had done. He said that I seemed to be a nice fellow, and that was all that mattered to him.

June came, and by this time I hated the Spruill Building. I had hated Central Prison, too, but when I weighed the pros and cons of the two places, I decided that the prison was a better place to be. At least you could smoke as much as you wanted there, and somehow the atmosphere wasn't as depressing.

Late in June I went back to Hillsborough for a pretrial hearing. My staff psychiatrist from the Spruill Building testified that I was, in her opinion, competent to stand trial. My attorneys didn't challenge this. They did challenge the admissibility of evidence obtained in a police search of my apartment, and Judge Battle granted their motion, adding that the evidence so obtained didn't add much to the case anyway.

My attorneys also moved that the trial and sentencing phases be held as separate proceedings, and the judge granted this motion as well. Afterward James Williams told me that this was very good, because it wouldn't put the jury in the position of determining my criminal responsibility and my sentence at the same time. "We don't want that," he said.

Many people, by the way, assured me that I had excellent attorneys. I still wasn't sure that I cared.

I returned to Central Prison, and was sent back to Mental Health East. I lit a cigarette at the first opportunity and reveled in my freedom to smoke. There were a few new faces on the ward, so I gave them Camel Lights and made friends quickly. There was no air conditioning, and everyone was sweltering in the summer heat. There was a large fan at one end of the day room, but it didn't help much. I settled fairly comfortably back into my old routine, and the days began to pass more quickly than they had at Dorothea Dix. My trial date had been set for October 23, so I began counting days. I actually believed at trial the truth would come out about how I was really a very nice guy who had been whipsawed by circumstances. On July 4 we each got a popsicle.

The inmate from New Jersey was still there, as were the Muslim and the 20-year-old larcenist with whom I had played spades and Monopoly. He always called the houses in Monopoly "crack houses," as in, "Give me another crack house on Park Place." It was really funny, to think of him spoiling every neighborhood into which he moved with rows of little green crack houses.

They told me the 16-year-old armed robber had gone to trial and gotten an 18-year sentence. I remembered that he had said that if he got more than five years he would commit suicide. I figured that boy's life was ruined, because he would learn nothing but criminal ways over a sentence that long, and he was already bad off enough.

I got fewer visits from my doctors and attorneys now that my evaluation at Dix was over. Dr. Bellard did tell me that the people at Dix were going to give the opinion that I was not criminally responsible. Based on what he had told me before, I guessed that I was now about one-quarter of the way through my incarceration, including both my prison and mental hospital stays.

That was assuming I would only be held in the mental hospital for a year or so. Kirk Osborn had told me it could easily be ten years, but that it was all up to me. If I obeyed the rules, took my medication, and went to all my activities, he said it could be considerably shorter. I was going to do everything I could to make it as short a stay as possible, and if one year in the hospital was the shortest possible, then one year it would be.

Dr. Bellard also told me that the particular antipsychotic medication I was taking would give me one advantage, because it could be given in shot form, called Haldol decanoate. This shot was time-released, and would be calculated to last for several weeks. Thus the authorities could make sure I was on my medication by making sure I showed up on the appointed days to take my shot. It would give me a considerable degree of freedom, and prevent everyone else a significant amount of worry.

In August I received a card from my father's old army buddies. About twenty of them had signed it, as well as some members of their families. I knew everyone, and almost cried again when I realized how good a bunch of guys those were.

Also that summer the Bosnian Serbs took the Muslim safe haven of Srebrenica and perpetrated the bloodiest massacre of the war there. Shortly thereafter, the powers that be decided they'd had enough, and began to bomb the Bosnian Serbs. Within a matter of weeks the Bosnian Serbs were at the bargaining table and the war was over. It all made me realize how right I had been to advocate attacking those aggressors back in 1992 and from then on. If people had listened to me, the war in Bosnia would never have gotten as bad as it did and thousands of people in Srebrenica would have been spared the atrocities that befell them, and yet here I was in the situation in which I now found myself for trying to do something to assert my own voice in such affairs. It seemed very ironic to me that I should be portrayed as the monster.

As always there was a constant influx of new inmates. I met one young man who said he had drunk a bottle of liquor called "Fighting Cock," blacked out, and woke up charged with one attempted murder and one attempted rape. He couldn't believe he was here. If I had learned my criminal law better, I would have remembered to tell him that because attempt is a specific-intent crime, voluntary intoxication constitutes a valid defense. I didn't recall that until much later, though. And even now I'm not sure if it's law in North Carolina.

Another inmate I liked said he had been a Green Beret medic for fifteen years. He had served all over the world, and was fascinating to talk to. He had a good head on his shoulders, and was only in the maximum-security prison because he had been given a 40-day contempt of court citation stemming from some troubles with his ex-wife, and when they had taken him to jail he started beating his head on the bars of his cell. "Adjust, adapt, and survive," he said he had been taught in the Army. His jailers thought he was crazy or suicidal, so he came to Mental Health East.

I also met an inmate nicknamed "Bullfrog." He was interesting, and later wrote a letter addressed to my parents' home that my father said was in some of the neatest handwriting he had ever seen. I don't remember what Bullfrog was charged with, but I hope he and all my other inmate friends fare well wherever they are, despite what they may have done in the past.

There is one new inmate who I know isn't faring well where he is. He told me that he was addicted to crack cocaine, and that when some dealers sold his daughter some crack he, knowing all too well how destructive that drug is, went to their house and killed three of them. He said people in the neighborhood were quoted in the newspapers that they were glad someone had had the guts to do something about the drug problem, but that they were sorry that it took people's getting killed. He told me he didn't want the death penalty, but more than a year later I saw on the news that that's what the jury gave him.

Even though there were inmates constantly coming and going, life in prison had a dreary sameness to it that was deadening to the senses. Spending fifty years here would be simply intolerable, I thought. The death penalty would be much better. I asked Mr. Hirsch if he thought I might get the death penalty, and he said Orange County, North Carolina hadn't given anyone the death penalty in decades. People there were too liberal for that, he said.

This was something I hadn't taken into account when trying to prove that people would be afraid to kill me. I wasn't afraid of death, but fifty years in prison! I again contemplated suicide, but the system goes to great lengths with people like me to keep us from doing that. That is something I don't understand. I think the penalty for murder should be death, as it is in some countries. Life in prison isn't as humane as death-penalty opponents seem to think it is, nor as civilized an alternative. It would be a punishment I would try to avoid with all my ability, though death would not have been.

Fall came, and as my trial date neared I got visitors from my former life. Bill came and told me about passing the Florida bar exam. He asked if I minded talking about things like that since my own chance at practicing law was gone, at least for the foreseeable future, and I said no. He also told me that the people from around the law school who had talked to the newspapers had been people who didn't really know me well, and that what they had said about me had been criticized by those who did. He said my real friends wouldn't talk to the newspapers for fear that it might somehow hurt my case.

My old friend from junior high school, Troy Dills, came and said that what I had done had really opened his eyes about what mental illness can do to someone. "I wish they could know you the way I did," he said. "It's just not something the Wendell I knew would have done. But don't you worry, they'll get this all straightened out and you'll get the help you need." I told him I had already gotten the help I need, and that since being on Haldol I hadn't had near the trouble from my illness that I had before the shooting, and that in fact I hadn't had even the slightest hallucination in the past few months. He seemed pleased.

Last came my friend from boarding school, Kevin Hicks. He was now in medical school at the Medical College of Virginia, after having graduated from William and Mary. We talked about the upcoming trial, and he said my attorneys wanted him to testify as a character witness. He asked if there was anything in particular I wanted him to say, and I said just to tell the truth. I figured that the truth was the only asset I had.

It seemed to take forever, but October 22 finally came. That evening a guard came to get me out of my cell. I was already packed and waiting for him. As we walked through the long prison corridors, he asked me where I was going. I said I was about to be tried for murder. He asked what I thought would happen, and I said that if I got convicted, I would probably get two life sentences plus about sixty years for assault charges.

"Good God!" he exclaimed.

Somehow the other inmates had gotten word of where I was headed, and strangers crowded around. "You're not leaving us, are you?" they asked. "You'll be back, won't you?" They seemed genuinely concerned that I might be leaving for good. It may sound hard to believe, but that's what I read in their faces and from their tones of voices. It was really sad, those poor guys.

Once again we headed down the road to Hillsborough, and once again I was quartered at the Orange County Jail. After supper the jailers brought in another prisoner to keep me company, and we sat up all night talking and smoking.

When morning came they came and got me, and I changed into my suit, with the leg brace underneath. A deputy drove me the short distance to the courthouse, and we passed many journalists and satellite television trucks. Much effort was being expended to cover my trial.

Inside the courthouse I met in a back room with my attorneys, and they gave me some last-minute advice. I was to stare straight ahead throughout the trial, and never make eye contact with the jurors. Where possible I was to lean forward with my head down. Under no circumstances was I to smile while in the courtroom. When I said I understood, Kirk said that he and James felt ready for what was to come.

I did my best to follow their instructions, with the result that I paid more attention to controlling my own demeanor than to what was going on in my trial, and I now remember little of what was said throughout it. Much of the time I just stared at the clock behind Judge Battle, or stared at the judge himself. Often he just stared back.

What I have since read about the two-week trial, though, has shown that most of the people I had spent so much effort talking to about my experiences and motives had nevertheless gleaned only the murkiest impression of either. The result was that the trial served to further distort my public image.

Also, I suppose my attorneys believed their only job was to get me acquitted, and that the way to do this was to play on jurors' stereotyped preconceptions about mental illness, e.g. that a person is insane only if his motives make no sense. This approach worked, but it also perpetuated the public's false impressions about me.

By the way, long after the trial was over I learned that the state could have saved enormous effort, time, and expense to have let a judge rather than a jury rule on the issue of insanity. In a less noto- rious case this probably would have been done. However, Carl Fox, the district attorney, was unwilling to allow a bench trial. The result was unnecessary negative publicity for me, which may have been Fox's goal all along.

As I have said, through most of the trial I stared straight ahead and paid little attention to the proceedings. There were a few exceptions—at one point I glanced at grisly photographs of the victims' corpses, and was horrified by what I had done to these men. However, I remembered that I had been trying to spare everyone else the same fate, and felt better. Also, during the doc- tors' testimony I could tell that they had gotten only the most gar- bled interpretation of my motives, and that this trial was therefore not going to help my public image at all.

During recesses, I talked with my attorneys and members of my family in a small room behind the courtroom. After Annetta testified she asked to see me, and we talked for a little while. She said that the whole thing had traumatized her, and asked me what would happen to me. I told her I would be fine. I also told my mother that if I got convicted I would try to get the death penal- ty, and my mother said she understood. That was a relief.

After closing arguments on the afternoon of Monday, November 6, the jury retired to deliberate and I got more time to visit with my family, my mother in particular. At one point I sent her out to get me a Coke, and when she came back with it she said that when the rest of my family saw her come out, they thought I had broken down under the pressure. I hadn't. I was trying to take a shortsighted view of my situation. The only immediate difference the verdict would make in my life was to determine where I would eat supper that night, and frankly the food at Central Prison was better than the food at Dorothea Dix. In fact, I remained so calm during this period that my father later said he was under the impression I was heavily sedated. I wasn't. I had just been through so much in the past four years that what was happening now seemed relatively minor in comparison.

On the morning of Tuesday, November 7, all of this continued. I talked with my mother in the back room for about half an hour and then someone came and said the jury was back with a verdict. Their deliberations had taken only two and a half hours. We all filed back into the courtroom, and the jury foreman passed a large envelope to Judge Battle. The judge opened it, leafed through a number of pages, and announced, "This says not guilty by reason of insanity." To me, he sounded surprised.

After the verdict was read, a deputy led me to the room behind the courtroom. He then went and got my mother. While he was gone, Kirk Osborn came in. As soon as the door closed behind him, he started jumping up and down and hitting me on the shoulder and saying "We beat this thing! We beat this thing!" It was by far the most excited I had ever seen him.

My mother came back, and she, too, was happy. "How do you feel?" she asked. I told her I was glad it had come out the way it had, but I was very aware that I was still in a very serious situation, and I still felt mortified by all that had happened. As I have said before, the only immediate difference the verdict would make was in where I would eat supper that night. We all talked for a while, but I don't remember saying much. When the conversation finally reached a lull, a deputy said it was time for me to go. I hugged my mother goodbye, thanked Kirk and James, and left. For the first time, the deputy didn't put handcuffs on me.

Outside I was mobbed by the press once more, but as usual I said nothing. We got into the deputy's car and rode past the crowd back to the jail. Inside, I changed out of my suit and into civilian clothes. I went back to my cell and asked my buddy if he'd heard the verdict yet, and he said, "Yeah, I heard you're crazier than a motherfucker." On television they were showing my senior informal picture from my high school yearbook and telling various things about my past. When they finished I said goodbye to my fellow prisoner and wished him luck, and he said goodbye and wished me luck, too. I then followed a deputy back to the car and we rode back to Raleigh. The deputy asked me if I was relieved, and I admitted that I was. I would have been lying to have said anything else, but still it was only a small part of myself that felt that way. The rest of me still felt mortified.

We drove once again to Dorothea Dix. As I sat in the waiting room with the deputy, the television was still talking about the verdict. After a time someone came and told me I was going back to the Spruill Building. This was discouraging but not surprising.

This time at the Spruill Building, though, I would have certain privileges. I could now wear my own clothes instead of state clothes, and I could keep big soft drinks in the refrigerator. I would not have to go to bed at any certain time. I was classified as a "crisis patient," and crisis patients didn't have to live by the same rules as the rest.

I was put on the ward parallel to my old ward, and I sat down in the day room to watch the other patients. At the usual smoke time, we all filed out onto the porch and lit cigarettes. I talked to some of the patients, and began once again to make new friends. I was back in the old routine.

Weeks passed. Now that it was late fall, we no longer went out into the exercise yard after supper. It was too cold, they said, so I had to do without that luxury. I continued to sleep late every day.

I got to know a man who had killed a man who was after his wife, he said. He had killed him with a single bullet to the head at a distance of about a hundred feet. "It was an accident, I swear," he said. Yeah, right, I thought, but I didn't say so. Really the man seemed pretty harmless, though, and I gravitated toward him. He was good company.

Another friend I made was there because he had pawned some of his parents' possessions to buy cocaine, and they had taken a warrant out on him. It was a violation of his parole or probation, I've forgotten which, and he was facing some significant time. One day I was talking to this individual in the hall, and a patient who was always getting into fights came up and pushed him. We had just been to the snack machines, and both of them had soft drinks. My friend threw his soft drink on the attacker, and the attacker threw his soft drink on my friend. They both started swinging, and one of the attacker's swings nearly hit me. I hit back, catching the attacker in the head. I broke my hand. The attacker then hit me in the head, breaking his hand.

For the next six weeks both of us had to wear casts. A lot of people thought that was really funny, but my psychiatrist told me I had better not get into any more fights if I wanted to be released. I paid attention, and since that time my record of behavior has been completely free of that sort of thing.

Speaking of getting released, in spite of myself I began asking my psychiatrist when she thought I would be released. I was thinking about my first commitment hearing, scheduled for fifty days after the trial ended. The outcome of my trial had led me to believe that society had determined not to punish me, but only to hold me for the protection of others until I was no longer dangerous. It was very clear to me that with my medication I was now no longer having the problems that had led to the shooting, and that I was absolutely not dangerous to anyone anymore.

There were at least two strong reasons why others should have believed me. First, the medication worked, and if I had been on medication before the shooting, the shooting wouldn't have happened. I needed constant reinforcement from the hallucinations to sustain my delusions, and without that, I wouldn't have done what I did ever in a million years. Second, now that I had done what I had done, I knew that it hadn't worked and that it wasn't going to work ever in the future. Just as I had never again gone around screaming and slapping my face to drive the alien thoughts out of my head again after being committed in 1992, and just as I never again went around videotaping people to prove my points as I had in 1994, I was destined never to again go around shooting people. None of those things had worked to my advantage, and so I never tried any of them again. I had absolutely no desire to go back to prison or to extend my stay in the mental hospital, and it seemed to me that everyone should see my reasons.

After all, my entire premise had been that if I was truly telepathic, those people would be afraid to shoot me. After it was over, I had to reassess—either I wasn't telepathic at all but rather mentally ill, or just because I was telepathic didn't mean they wouldn't shoot to wound. Either way, it was a course of action which it would be unthinkable for me to repeat.

My psychiatrist said that I would be a patient for a long time, and that by this she meant for more than one year. She said that it would take more than one year for me to prove that I was no longer dangerous. I said that it would soon be more than one year since the shooting, and that in that time I had not become delusional a single time. Furthermore, with my medication now being stabilized, I was not apt to ever become dangerous again. She said that even with the year just past, it would still take more than one year for me to prove what I had to prove in order to be released. We argued, and she won.

Still, I wanted out. I knew I wasn't dangerous. My hearing was scheduled for December 27. As December wore on and there was no word from a lawyer, I began to worry what would happen if they didn't get the hearing done in time. My psychiatrist assured me that I would have the hearing, and that they couldn't hold me if there wasn't one. Finally, a few days before Christmas, my attorney showed up. His name was Karl Knudsen, and he said that he had had the hearing rescheduled for January 12. I protested that this was more than a fifty-day period after my trial, and that they had no right to hold me past December 27. He said that the period could be extended if the patient agreed, and that he had agreed for me. I thought, and still think, that this was a violation of my rights.

At about that time, my mother and my cousin Charlie Williamson came to visit. They brought food, and we had a good time despite the circumstances. All through the visit, though, I was preoccupied with the thought that there were now two people who would never again spend Christmas with their families, and all because of me. It was definitely enough to put a gloom on my holiday spirit.

I spent Christmas and New Year's at the Spruill Building, and I thought about how much more fun I had had over the previous year's holidays in New England, now seemingly so long ago. I wondered if I would ever enjoy myself like that again. For a Christmas present the hospital gave everyone a package with things like socks, deodorant, and shampoo in it. Mine also had a coloring book.

In January I learned that I was soon to be transferred from the forensic unit to a rehabilitation unit. My psychiatrist recommended Broughton Hospital in Morganton, North Carolina, but Karl Knudsen said that would be a bad idea. "Dorothea Dix would be a much better place for you to be," he said. "We've worked really hard to get opportunities here for people in your legal category." He said that Dorothea Dix would be so much better for me than Broughton that it would even outweigh the consideration that

Broughton was a three-hour drive closer to my family.

He also said that if I insisted on having a commitment hearing I could have one, but that I would have zero chance of being released at that time and that having the hearing would only stir up more resentment against me among the public. He said that my fate would largely be determined by politics and public opinion, and recommended waiving the hearing at this time. After much deliberation I agreed.

My next chance would be in ninety days, which meant April. If my hearing had been in December like it was supposed to be, then ninety days would have ended in March instead. My attorney had just cost me a month in the mental hospital. I got pretty bent out of shape about that, and made a lot of angry telephone calls home to complain. My parents sympathized, and said that they had hoped that after the verdict I would be put in a more therapeutic environment than I had been in before, or was in now. They could tell that I was miserable.

Just when things were at their lowest, two of my old law school buddies came to visit me at Spruill, Bill and Paul Koutouzakis. They brought me a pizza. They seemed genuinely relieved about the verdict and told me that they were hoping I would be released soon. I told them that I was hoping for the same thing, but that things weren't looking too good. My doctors had said that my belief that I might be released in a short time showed that I was out of touch with reality, and yet here were two perfectly sane and healthy people who shared my optimism. It made me believe that the doctors just interpreted things however they wanted to, and were not above putting their own overly dire interpretation on anything I said or did. I really enjoyed visiting with Bill and Paul, though, and was very glad they had come.

Because I was now able to wear civilian clothes, I had my mother bring me some. I had gained twenty pounds in prison, unfortunately, and my jeans no longer fit. I had to send her out to buy a larger size. It was nice being able to wear my own clothes again, and I felt better with them on.

On January 26, 1996, my name was in the news again because it was the first anniversary of the shooting. They had interviews with various people in Chapel Hill who remembered the incident and the effect it had had on their lives. A patient who was watching with me, whom I won't describe except to say that my attorney had warned me to stay away from him because he was big, crazy, and dangerous, started saying, "You weren't thinking when you did that, man. You just weren't thinking." I got mad because I knew that was the common perception, and it was wrong, and I told this individual that I had been thinking plenty and that he didn't know what he was talking about. He just kept repeating that I hadn't been thinking, and I had to leave the room before I got into trouble for fighting again.

That patient, by the way, was one of only two killers I've met, out of dozens, who I considered to be bad people. This particular one had killed someone on the outside, had been found not guilty by reason of insanity, and then had killed another mental patient while he was there in the hospital.

The other killer I had no respect for was someone who had killed for money and was in the process of trying to deny having done it. Those are the only two who I feel really deserve the fate I think they have coming to them.

Something that had really irritated me ever since the shooting was when people said "You're lucky the police didn't kill you" or "You're lucky to be alive." I personally believe that death is by far not the worst thing that can happen to a person, and there were many times when I felt like I had gotten the short end of the stick by surviving the shooting.

Old friends left and new ones came. I met a man who had killed his girlfriend in front of her young child, and wanted the death penalty. He said he no longer had the will or the desire to live, and that he deserved to die. He sought me out because he had heard that I'd been to law school, and he wanted advice on how to get the death penalty. I was unable to help him, but I did point out that his lawyers would be "ethically" bound to secure the "best" deal for him that they could. Therefore, unless there were strong aggravating factors against him, he would have an uphill battle in getting executed. I wished him luck, though, and told him I knew how he felt. He seemed like a nice guy, really.

I spent a lot of time with two other men. One of these had been with several other teenagers who had gone into an elderly couple's house to rob them, and ended up stabbing both nearly to death. He said he hadn't known anyone was going to get hurt, and that he hadn't been the one to do the stabbing, but that he had tried to leave the state with the others. They had gotten nearly as far as Texas before being stopped for speeding, and then extradited back to North Carolina to face numerous charges. They had been labeled a "Satanic cult" by the local news media.

The other man was in less trouble. He had been accused of trying to run a police officer off the road one night, and he said that he just hadn't seen the officer's car. He had been taking medication for a number of bee stings at the time, and as more time passed it had begun to look like the authorities would treat that as an involuntary intoxication which would excuse him from criminal liability.

The three of us hung around together until February 20, and then I was transferred to a rehab unit there at Dix. My new home would be Lineberger Building, Ward C. I had really been looking forward to this move, and truly hoped it would bring me a big step closer to getting out. After all, I was no longer delusional or dangerous, and it seemed that anyone would be able to see this. I thought that the doctors in the forensic unit were probably biased against me, or would at least be reluctant to recommend my release after having argued so recently that at the time of the shooting, I had not been in full control of my faculties. Surely, I thought, I would get a fairer shake in a rehab unit.

On February 20 I packed up my belongings and carried them through the gates to a hospital van waiting outside. It was a cold, rainy morning, but I was in a good mood because I was finally leaving the Spruill Building for what I was sure would be the last time. We drove down the hill to Lineberger, and then I carried my things inside and was processed in. We then went upstairs to Ward C.

There I met my new psychiatrist, Dr. Wouters. Georgia Tech's basketball team was playing someone on the television there in the day room, and after I was introduced to the doctor I made a remark about Georgia Tech's prospects.

"No, that's not right," said Dr. Wouters, and then rephrased exactly what I had said as if he were setting me straight. It was not the last time I was to get the feeling that we weren't communicating effectively, and this was to be a constant shadow over our relationship.

I met a patient who remembered having seen me at the Spruill Building. He introduced himself and showed me around the ward, explaining how life was there. He told me he was waiting to be tried for stealing a few cartons of cigarettes, which would be a parole violation and could get him a ten-year sentence. I couldn't imagine doing ten years in prison over a few measly cartons of cigarettes, but the justice system is strange sometimes.

He was a tall, very gaunt man, and suffered from depression. Sometimes he would be so depressed that he didn't want to talk to anyone, but he would always have a few kind words for me. We became pretty good friends as the next few months passed, and I was sorry on the day that the police came and led him away in handcuffs and shackles. I have since often wondered if he really got the ten years he was dreading.

While the two of us were getting to know one another, I was

also learning about life in Lineberger Ward C. It didn't take long to figure out that if I was any better off here than in Spruill, it wasn't by much. The best thing was that it was less crowded. The worst thing was that the patients were in worse shape mentally, and the staff was just as unfriendly as those in Central Prison or the Spruill Building had been.

An illustration. One day after lunch we were sitting around in the day room watching "Hogan's Heroes" on television. A nurse came in and turned off the TV.

"Hey, what's the big idea?" somebody wanted to know.

"We're going to have a medication education class," she said.

"You're not using me for a damn guinea pig," someone else said.

More people chimed in. "When am I getting out of here?"

"Last night Jesus cut off my head and shot laser beams up my ass."

The nurse held up her hand. "Please be quiet," she said. "Tell that to the doctor. We're going to discuss psychotropic medications today. Some people have confused thinking and need these medications to help them think more clearly."

"Then Jesus posed as my voice and forged a bunch of bad checks and stole my limousines."

"I'm going to court in eight months and then I'm getting out of here. I'm tired of this place."

"I'm gonna go home and beat my wife."

"No more interruptions," the nurse said. She went on with her class, with constant off-the-wall interruptions.

"Have you ever been to Detroit?"

"Do you know Zeke somebody who owns a gas station in Vance County?"

Still the nurse went on. She concluded by saying that these medications made some people constipated, so next week we would talk about laxatives.

"My bowels are burning me up."

"I've seen Jesus in other solar systems in other galaxies. He has a briefcase full of MY MONEY!"

The nurse asked if anyone could tell her what we'd been over, so I gave her a brief synopsis and she thanked me and left.

"What did she want?" somebody asked.

I include this part not to make fun of mentally ill people, but to show what my life was like then and has been ever since.

Another thing I didn't like about Ward C was that we had to get up at 6:30 every morning 365 days a year. If we didn't get a shower between 8:00 a.m. and 9:00 a.m., then we didn't get a shower that day. That struck me as absolutely ridiculous and even a little mean. Sometimes I overslept, and then they would write that I had poor hygiene in my psychiatric records, as if I didn't have enough sense to take a shower every day.

After I had been on Ward C for about a month, one day I asked Dr. Wouters what his plans for me were as far as eventual discharge. He seemed surprised that I would even ask, and said that it would be at least ten years. "Nobody is going to be in any hurry to see you back on the streets," he said.

Ten years! But what about my medication? How could they justify holding someone in a mental hospital who had long ago ceased to suffer from mental problems?

Dr. Wouters said that he doubted very seriously that I no longer suffered from mental problems, and when I asked him what evidence he had, he said that he had seen me sitting quietly and that I "might have been hearing voices."

I told him that I hadn't been hearing voices, which was the truth, but he said that it would still be at least ten years before I might be released. "Maybe longer," he said. He told me about a fairly recent case in which someone in a legal situation similar to mine had been released and had done well, but had been attacked by someone and killed his attacker in self-defense. Even though he was acquitted at trial on self-defense, the family of the man he had killed had sued the hospital that released him and had won. Dr. Wouters said that this case would tend to keep people like myself in the hospital indefinitely.

Later I told a nurse what he had said, and she said that it was still better than being in prison for the rest of my life.

As months passed and Dr. Wouters still didn't budge from his ten-year expected time frame, I began to get very depressed again, and wished I was dead. However, a mental hospital is by design a very difficult place in which to commit suicide, so this option was effectively denied me. Once again I hated God, and once again felt frustrated because I didn't believe a God existed for me to hate. I also thought often of the two men I had killed but who, horrifyingly, hadn't deserved to die at all, and of their families.

Once, when I was talking to Dr. Wouters about his idea of holding me in the hospital for ten years, he asked me if I had ever heard the legend of Sisyphus. I said that Sisyphus was a figure from ancient Greek mythology who had been condemned to spend eternity in the lowest region of the underworld, where he had to always push to the top of a hill a huge stone that always rolled back down.

Dr. Wouters said, "Yes, but what you didn't mention, and I think it's very significant that you failed to mention it, is the fact that Sisyphus was entirely at peace with himself and his fate." He told me that I could learn a lot from Sisyphus.

That night I told my mother what Dr. Wouters had said, and she said she first of all had never heard that Sisyphus was entirely at peace with himself and his fate, and second, that Dr. Wouters was entirely out of line to compare my situation with that of Sisyphus. She thought it was a bad practice of medicine.

However, since that time I have come to think of Dr. Wouters' conception of Sisyphus to be an apt metaphor for my fate.

I talked to my parents on the telephone frequently, and they encouraged me to focus on the positive. They thought that now that I had been acquitted, there was still a chance that I might earn my UNC law degree. In March 1996 my mother contacted Kirk Osborn about challenging the indefinite suspension into which I had been placed on the day of the shooting. He agreed to look into it, and said that if I should happen to be readmitted, that they would have to make "reasonable accommodations" for me, which he thought would mean allowing me to finish my last three courses while still in the hospital. This was pursuant to the Americans With Disabilities Act of 1990.

For a time Kirk seemed quite optimistic about my chances in this area, and so when in April Karl Knudsen again suggested that I waive my commitment hearing and accept another six months in the hospital, I agreed, because I thought I might be able to complete my law degree during that time. Karl didn't have the order entered until May, though, which cost me yet another month of hospital time.

Also in May a committee at UNC met with Kirk and my mother, and the University purported to "prove" that I was still dangerous to others and therefore not acceptable to the University community. Thus they never had to address the fact that I could take my courses while still in the hospital, and therefore could not possibly pose a danger to anyone in the University community.

What really galled me about this finding was that I knew I was not dangerous to anyone any longer, and yet they had supposedly proven that I was. It was determined at the hearing that the University had the burden of proof on this issue. They had therefore "proven" something that wasn't true. I wonder even now when they expect this supposed dangerousness to assert itself.

I tried to do everything right. I was assigned to two activities which I attended every week. One was Music Therapy, and it involved playing rock music along with other mentally ill musicians. That was fun. The woman who led the group was a wonderful, beautiful person, and I greatly admired her for choosing to make helping others less fortunate her life's work, because with her brains and talent she could have been doing any number of other jobs that would have paid more.

My other activity was Occupational Therapy. It involved making ceramics. I got bored with it immediately, but if painting ceramic mushrooms would help me get out of the hospital any sooner, then I would be the best damn ceramic mushroom painter I could be. I often wondered, as I sat there painting ceramic mushrooms, what this could possibly have to do with treating someone who had done what I had done. What does shooting people have to do with ceramic mushrooms? Why did this have to happen to me?

It wasn't that the occupational therapists didn't care. In fact, they recommended that I participate in a 3-day activity called AIM (Adventure Into Me), which turned out to be the highlight of an unremarkable summer. The activity was designed to build confidence and teamwork through group problem-solving, all using rock-climbing equipment. The other participants were high-functioning patients, and the whole thing turned out to be pretty fun, though it really didn't teach me anything I hadn't learned as a teenager in Boy Scouts. At least it was an excuse to get outside.

Not that I needed one. Every day the techs on Ward C made sure we spent several hours sitting out in the fenced exercise yard beside Lineberger. This would have been a good idea except that as the summer wore on we began to roast in the sun, and there was nothing to do but put up with the nerve-shattering foibles of some of the sicker patients. This exercise yard had even less to offer than the yard beside the Spruill Building had. Also, even though we were outside, here we weren't allowed to smoke any more than our usual ration of two cigarettes every two hours.

I had no one to talk to really, but I did befriend one patient who seemed to be not quite as delusional as the others. He had killed his girlfriend and been found incompetent to stand trial because of his schizophrenia, and he was friendly, though not the most scintillating of conversationalists. In fact, it was hard to get him to say three words in a row. He appeared to have no aspirations other than to spend the rest of his life in a mental hospital, but he was the best I could find, so he was who I talked to when I needed to talk. All in all, it was an awful summer.

Dorothea Dix Hospital, as I have mentioned before, is right across the street from Central Prison, and there is a constant flow of people, both inmates and staff, between the two. I was frequently running into people at Dix who I had seen at the prison, and at least one of the techs on my ward was a former prison guard. I am not sure that this is a good thing or a bad thing, but I do think it is a thing that people should be aware of and think about. Also, it made my "treatment" at Dix seem a lot more like punishment than I believe was theoretically intended for people in my legal situation. Then again, sometimes I think punishment is the goal after all, at least to some.

On the evening news one night I saw a story about Demetrise Stephenson, the police officer I had wounded on that terrible day nearly two years earlier. She was no longer able to continue her police work because of the disability that resulted from her being shot in the hand, but she had begun a program of helping young people in high-crime areas keep their lives straight. She said she enjoyed her new line of work, and that she was planning to pursue a career as a police detective at some point in the future. I was sorry to have injured a person of such apparently good character, but even more than that I was glad she was taking the initiatives that she had and that things appeared to be working out for her.

One of my fellow patients told me that they had seen her on the news, too, and that she had said she held no ill will toward me and that she hoped things worked out for me, too. This was nice to hear, but since I didn't see it myself I have no way of knowing if it's true or if it was just another delusion this fellow had dreamed up. I may never know.

In the summer of 1996 Vladimir Zhirinovsky took a beating in the Russian presidential election and Boris Yeltsin was re-elected.

I was glad, as I'm certain a lot of other Americans were, but I no longer cared as much as I once had. The world was changing. Even Yitzhak Rabin, the Israeli head of state whose 1993 peace agreement with the PLO had put me on edge about the fulfillment of Biblical prophecy and the end of the world, was dead. He had been assassinated at the time of my murder trial by, of all people, a third-year Israeli law student.

At my trial I had been served notice of a wrongful-death civil lawsuit against my family and myself by the victims or their families. All through my stay at Dix I was involved in defending myself against that suit, or rather, in helping my parents' homeowners' insurer to defend me. For a time I considered filing for bankruptcy, but I learned that even that measure probably wouldn't help me if a judgment were rendered against me.

The company which defended us was State Farm, and they did a fine job as far as I was concerned. First, they didn't insure against intentional acts, but they ruled mine to have been an unintentional act. Second, the policy only covered members of the household in which my parents lived, and I hadn't lived with them full time in years. However, my parents did keep my old room for me, which the State Farm adjusters inspected. State Farm then decided that I was a member of the household and therefore covered by the policy.

These cases dragged on for months, but finally in the fall of 1996 State Farm reached a settlement with the plaintiffs which absolved us all from further liability. This was a tremendous relief for us, and I am greatly indebted to that company for its services.

One day I mentioned to a fellow patient, who I had known for several months, why I was in the hospital.

"Oh my God!" he said. "That was you? Oh my God! Oh my God!" He had read all about it in the newspapers. When he finally recovered from his shock, he said, "Man, the newspapers made you out to be some kind of nerd or something. You're not at all like I expected you to be from that. It's like two different people. I would never have even known it was you, if you hadn't just told me."

When I tried to be completely objective about it, I decided that at least half of the staff I had met at Dix were pretty decent people, but there were still enough bad attitudes around to give the place its unwholesome, even hostile, atmosphere. Every patient, no matter how sick or out of touch with reality, agreed that Dix was a bad place to be, and even my family soon picked up on it and commented on it.

However, it wasn't until the fall of 1996 that I learned that this hostile atmosphere was not common to all state mental hospitals. That was when Ward C got a new patient, which incidentally was an extreme rarity because most of our patients stayed for years and years. This new patient had transferred from Broughton Hospital to Dix because his family had moved to Raleigh, and as soon as he realized how big a difference there was between the two hospitals he began telling me about it.

"This place sucks, Wendell," he said. "If you ever get a chance to transfer to Broughton, take it. That place has this place beat in every category."

He seemed like a pretty reasonable person, and I soon began to wonder if he was right. The more he told me about Broughton, the more I began to see that it would be a much better place for me, in spite of what Karl Knudsen had said. Therefore, when my next commitment hearing came up later in the fall, I told Karl that I would not challenge my commitment if he would get me transferred to Broughton to be closer to my family. He agreed, and though it took him from mid-November until the end of December to make the order effective, I finally got my transfer approved. Of course, as with the two previous opportunities for a commitment hearing, I lost at least a month of additional hospital time. That made a total of three months I would have to spend unnecessarily in the hospital, just because my attorney was slow to get papers filed.

"As a practical matter it makes no difference," he told my mother, but she knew as well as I did that if it had been Karl Knudsen sitting on Ward C in that atmosphere for three extra months, it would make plenty of difference. I was mad, but there was nothing I could do about it.

Over Thanksgiving weekend Paul Koutouzakis came to visit me, and he brought us each a turkey sub to celebrate the holiday. He told me he was now living in Atlanta, was still looking for a permanent job, and that he had been to a World Series game when the Braves hosted the Yankees. It was a really good visit, and I was glad he had been thoughtful enough to come. Friends who will continue to stick by you even when the chips are down are hard to find.

In early December an order came down that all people who were in North Carolina state mental hospitals because they were charged with a crime or were found not guilty by reason of insanity could only leave their wards if accompanied by staff on a one-to-one basis, unless they had a specific court order to the contrary. This was because there had been several escapes in recent months.

Before this rule came down, we had been allowed to go out in groups of five if we had one staff member. Thus, though the vast majority of us had done nothing wrong while in the hospital, we were all restricted. I had to quit going to my activities.

For Christmas 1996 I again received a package from the hospital which contained socks, deodorant, and a small bottle of cheap but pungent cologne. This time, however, there was no coloring book, which disappointed me. I learned from staff that the cologne contained no alcohol because patients in years past had been drinking the stuff.

In early January Dr. Wouters made one last effort to sabotage me by having a team of mental health experts come from UNC (of all places) to evaluate me. They interviewed me, and ordered a battery of psychological tests which they then interpreted in as negative a light as possible.

With these out of the way, I transferred to Broughton on January 22. I spent an afternoon on an admissions ward, and then they took me to a long-term rehab unit in Harper Building. The tech who processed me into Harper Ward 24 said, "Things are pretty laid back around here." That was good to hear.

I quickly came to realize that I had made a good decision to transfer to Broughton. Some of the patients were friendly and in pretty good shape mentally, and the staff without exception had good attitudes about their work. I met the Program Director, a psychologist named Dr. Woodruff, and was impressed. After he had known me for a while, and after he had seen the results of the most recent battery of tests I had taken at Dorothea Dix he told me, "Those people are paranoid about you, and they're just trying to transfer some of that paranoia up here with you."

For the most part, my nearly two years in Harper Building went pretty well. I participated in a horticulture group led by two fine fellows named Chuck Lowdermilk and Rip Barrier, which allowed me to get outside into the garden one afternoon a week. I used to walk three times a week with a pretty woman who was also a good conversationalist, but the powers that be decided that she had better things to do than walk me, so they discontinued me from that program. I took music therapy, and I worked as a video-tape technical assistant in a studio at the hospital library. Most important, I participated in a schizophrenia support group, where I learned a great deal about the illness which afflicts me. No one at Dorothea Dix ever made such an effort to help me understand my illness.

I learned that my particular form of schizophrenia is caused by an excess of the neurotransmitter dopamine. Dopamine facilitates the firing of neurons, and when there is too much of it, neurons fire which aren't supposed to. The result is all of the hallucinations which I described in the first section of this book. Haldol is a dopamine inhibitor, and in the proper dosages it prevents the firing of neurons which aren't supposed to fire. Thus, as long as I take Haldol, my dopamine level will remain proper and I will have no hallucinations, and without hallucinations, I will not become delusional.

The opposite of schizophrenia is Parkinson's Disease, in which there is a lack of dopamine. People on medication for schizophrenia sometimes display symptoms of Parkinson's, while people on medication for Parkinson's sometimes display symptoms of schizophrenia.

The typical age of onset for schizophrenia is the late teens to the early twenties. Mine first showed up when I was 23. No one knows for sure what causes schizophrenia, but researchers suspect a genetic link. By the way, no one, myself included, believes my singing so intensely could have caused the illness, though singing could certainly have caused the pains in my head and abdomen.

I met other patients who had been to the Spruill Building, and they all agreed that Dorothea Dix was a terrible place to be. One of them said he had been solicited for oral sex by one of the male staff there, and another said that when he tried to draw his weekly allowance of $25, the tech who was giving out the money told him to sign first and then walked away with the patient's money. When the patient complained, they simply told him he shouldn't have signed first.

Nothing quite like that ever happened to me, but I'd seen enough out of some of those people at Dix that I believed it.

Of course, life wasn't perfect at Broughton, either. People who think I was living a country club existence there couldn't be more wrong. If they had to live among some of the worst cases of mental illness in the state, and abide by the rules designed for such people, they would know what I mean.

In the summer of 1997 I had a therapist who I told about a particular Nirvana song which I considered famous, but which she said she had never heard.

"You'll hear it if you live long enough," I assured her.

"What do you mean, 'if I live long enough?'" she asked.

I told her I meant no harm, and that what I had said was just an expression meant to cover the uncertainties of life, but I later learned that she had written in my chart that I was making "veiled threats" on her life. That's how careful I have to be about what I say.

Also, in September 1997 Dr. Woodruff accepted a job in another part of the state, and with him I lost a valuable ally. His temporary replacement ordered yet another battery of psychological tests for me to take, which were once again interpreted in what appeared to me to be the most pessimistic light possible. For that reason my December 1997 commitment hearing was something of a disappointment, though Kirk Osborn (whom my parents had privately retained to represent me) did arrange for me not to be transferred back to the new forensic unit at Dorothea Dix, which was a move that had been contemplated by the authorities.

By the way, on my way back to Broughton after that hearing, I got to know a deputy sheriff named Dave Hill who used to work for the Chapel Hill police department. In fact, he had loaned his patrol car to Demetrise Stephenson on the day of the shooting.

"That doesn't make you uncomfortable, does it?" he asked.

"Frankly, yes it does," I said.

He then told me he had no hard feelings, that he didn't take things like that personally, and that he always tried to take a professional attitude toward his work. He was very nice, in other words. When I got back to Broughton I met with my parents and told them about him, and they said everyone in the Chapel Hill police department had been very polite and considerate to them, much as he had been toward me. My mother added that it was quite a contrast from the attitudes of certain members of the UNC-CH administration with whom she had had contact, and

who she said had acted like "horses' rear ends" about the whole
thing.

On the advice of several people familiar with my case, through
attorney Nick Gordon in April 1997 I sued UNC and Dr. Liptzin
for negligence. Details of these lawsuits could fill another book,
and I am probably not the one to write it. However, the gist of our
case was that Dr. Liptzin had implied that I could stop taking
Navane and still expect to make a rational decision about whether
to begin taking it again should the need arise. As we have seen, a
rational decision like that ceased to be within my power after I
stopped taking the medication. Also, Dr. Liptzin failed to make
plans for that foreseeable contingency, and I suffered badly as a
result.

At any rate, the case against Dr. Liptzin went to trial in
September 1998. After nearly six days of testimony and two days
of deliberations, the jury returned a $500,000 verdict in my favor.
Surprisingly to me, this set off another media storm. Highly sen-
sationalized accounts of the lawsuit were reported by, among others, the New York Times, "Time" magazine, and CBS's "60
Minutes." I will spare you the details, but throughout the furor
some of the jurors themselves became determined advocates for
my cause. I remain deeply indebted to them for their help.

Unfortunately for my financial situation, however, the state
immediately began placing liens against the judgment to pay for
my hospital care at over $300 a day, retroactive to 1995. Again,
this took Nick and me by surprise, and after he researched the subject he said there is nothing we can do about it. Thus, as I understand it, I would never have seen a penny of that $500,000, nor
will I benefit financially from this book.

In December, 2000, the North Carolina Court of Appeals
ruled that despite his negligence, Dr. Liptzin could not be held
accountable, and thus they overturned the jury's decision.

In November 1998 I was caught at Broughton drinking contraband vodka, and ostensibly for that reason in December 1998 I was transferred to the forensic unit at Dorothea Dix. However, I am not alone in believing the real reason for the transfer was to retaliate for my attorneys' winning that lawsuit. Petitions advocating my transfer had been circulating long before the drinking incident. Nevertheless, I was wrong to break the rules, so I guess I gave them all the excuse they needed.

I will say nothing about my life in the forensic unit, because if I say something good about it, the public will want to crack down, and if I say something bad, then the psychologists and social workers here will say I am not adjusting properly. Besides, I'm tired of complaining. I've had my say.

In October 1999, I received a letter from a woman named Amy Martin, who said that she had written her English Master's thesis criticizing the media's coverage of my criminal case. She had successfully defended the thesis in June 1999, and later let me read it. It was a thought-provoking piece of writing, and I agreed with her conclusions and encouraged her to have the thesis published. She still visits me frequently, and we have become good friends.

In December 1999 I was again denied grounds privileges, even though my treatment team was strongly in support of my having them. In court much was made of misleading items in my chart, such as the fact that in September I had been observed talking to myself. Actually, I was memorizing song lyrics I had written, but I wasn't in court to tell anyone that, so it looked bad.

However, by this point my expectations were low and my disappointment in the results of the hearing was mild.

As I come to the end of this book there are certain things which I still feel the need to say. First, my medication works in ways I never would have anticipated a few years ago. I am no longer tormented by my brater. I am no longer paranoid. Even my left shoulder, which bothered me for so long while I was psychotic, feels like its old self now. I am also a member of Alcoholics Anonymous, and I have no intention of ever using drugs or alcohol in the future. There is every reason in the world to think that I would be able to resume a normal life to the extent that other people let me.

However, I am no longer under any illusions about that ever happening. I have been told that the statute under which I was committed mandates that a person is to be considered dangerous if he or she has committed an act of violence in the "relevant past," which I take to mean that I won't be released until some time in the irrelevant future. Ever since the State of North Carolina shifted the burden of proof on whether a defendant like myself is dangerous or not, no person found not guilty by reason of insanity for the crime of murder in a high-profile case like mine has been released from a state mental hospital, regardless of how good a case they were able to present to show they are no longer dangerous. Also, my problems won't end even if I should someday be released. I have come to see myself as my lawyers seem to see me, as a person whose fate will be controlled more by politics and public opinion than by good medicine.

Needless to say, with all the negative publicity I have generated I do not expect to be released in as little as ten years. It could easily be twenty, thirty, or the rest of my life. That is something I have to accept, the price I have to pay. Like Sisyphus I have adapted, am adapting, and will continue to adapt. What happened on Henderson Street in Chapel Hill on January 26, 1995 has become a part of my sense of who I am, now and always.

Not surprisingly, in the years after the shooting my attitude about what happened has evolved into something considerably different from the way I viewed it immediately afterward, or even when I wrote much of this book. Even in the earliest days of my confinement I viewed the shooting as a terrible tragedy for all concerned. However, I believed my action had been essentially rational, and that attitude colored much of this book. I thought other people didn't understand my belief because they had never been in my shoes, so all the sufferings I experienced in those days I took with an attitude of heroic martyrdom.

Now, though, I cannot see anything rational, let alone heroic, about what I did. Even if things had been precisely as I imagined them to be at the time of the shooting—i.e., even in the extremely unlikely event that I had really been broadcasting my thoughts to the whole word and even if the world had been wronging me and each other in the ways I perceived—there was nothing rational or heroic about the "solution" I chose. There was no sane reason to believe that by resorting to violence, even in those extreme circumstances, I could do anything but make a bad situation worse. There was no sane reason, in other words, to expect the outcome to have been any different than it turned out.

That is how I explain the situation to myself now. I do not know why it took me so long to see this, but I have been told my lack of insight was probably as biologically-based as my delusions and hallucinations were.

Finally, and most importantly, I need to say something about my feelings for the families of Ralph Walker and Kevin Reichardt. The fact that I haven't said more on the subject doesn't mean I don't think about them every day and will probably always do so.

I cannot know what these families feel because what happened to them has never happened to me. I do know that my actions caused them a devastating loss that can never be made up. No one who hasn't been in my situation could know how hurtful this is. At any rate, I wish I could find a way to express the sorrow and compassion I feel without saying so much as to be accused of wearing my remorse on my sleeve, or of not meaning what I say.

I got the impression that initiating contact with these families would be a bad idea. Kirk said it might take my having children of my own to understand the impact of what I had done.

I just wish I could go back to 1992 knowing what I know now, and it would all be different for everyone involved. I wish I had gotten on the Haldol shot at the first sign of trouble, and never slid down that slippery slope of psychosis. Ironically, I needed to be on the medication and advised to stay on it for life before I could see the true need to do so, and that never happened until it was far too late. I just can't get over my disbelief that all of this had to happen to me.

And for the people whose lives I have ruined, I will be forever sorry.